VIKRAMORVASHIYAM

KALIDASA

VIKRAMORVASHIYAM

Quest for Urvashi

Translated from the Sanskrit by
A.N.D. Haksar

PENGUIN BOOKS
An imprint of Penguin Random House

PENGUIN BOOKS

USA | Canada | UK | Ireland | Australia
New Zealand | India | South Africa | China

Penguin Books is part of the Penguin Random House group of companies
whose addresses can be found at global.penguinrandomhouse.com

Published by Penguin Random House India Pvt. Ltd
7th Floor, Infinity Tower C, DLF Cyber City,
Gurgaon 122 002, Haryana, India

First published in Penguin Books by Penguin Random House India 2021

ISBN 9780670093632

Typeset in Adobe Garamond Pro by Manipal Technologies Limited, Manipal
Printed at Replika Press Pvt. Ltd, India

www.penguin.co.in

P.M.S.

For my son
Vikram
with all my love

Contents

Introduction

The play *Vikramorvashiyam* by Kalidasa is here presented in a new translation for modern readers. Its original source and setting are perhaps the oldest among all three of this famous writer's existing dramatic works. The source is a hymn (10.95) from the *Rig Veda* itself. That was followed in Vedic literature by a more elaborate retelling in the *Shatapatha Brahmana* (5.1–2). Later, there were versions with further details and changes in the Sanskrit idiom of Puranic literature. Of these, the most notable are in the *Matsya* (24.10–32), *Padma* (12.62–68) and *Bhagavata* (IX.14–47) Puranas, all with additions or changes to the original story. Kalidasa then created his own with further embellishments.[i] While this literary evolution is not traced here as a whole, its beginning in the *Rig Veda* is touched on later to provide some original background to this play.

The setting of this play is neither just the celestial world of heavenly beings nor only the earthly one of humankind. It is, in the words of the celebrated scholar, philosopher and second President of India, Dr S. Radhakrishnan, 'a blend of the human and the superhuman'. The respected European Sanskritist Maurice Winternitz described it as 'a narrative drama in which mortal beings have active and reciprocal communication with gods and demi-gods,' here recounted in 'lyrico–dramatic poetry, half show-play, half opera'.[ii]

The play's hero, Pururavas, is an earthly ruler, though with a genealogy that featured some celestial ancestors. The heroine, Urvashi, is an apsara, a divine nymph from heaven. The dramatic action includes participants and dialogues from both heaven and earth. Some ancient commentators have categorized this play as a *trotaka*, a type in which humans and celestials act together and intermingle.[iii]

*

Before discussing the play, one may start with some words about its author. Kalidasa is at present the best-known and most written about poet and dramatist from ancient India. Recent scholarship places him in the fourth to fifth century CE, at the height of the Gupta Empire, in a peak period of ancient India's courtly culture. Nothing is known of his life or person though there are some picturesque but contradictory legends. What is well known and extolled are his still-existing works: three plays, two epic poems and two that are lyrical. These have also established his fame in the wider world of letters.[iv]

Kalidasa entered this wider, modern Western world through an English translation over two hundred years ago. This was of his play *Abhijnanashakuntalam*, by a British East India Company official, Sir William Jones, that appeared in 1789. It earned praise from prominent European literary figures of the time, like Goethe, Herder and Schiller, leading to further translations of Kalidasa's other works in various languages in the following century. The first English translation of *Vikramorvashiyam*, by the Oxford professor of Sanskrit M. Monier-Williams, appeared in 1849. Three decades later, there was another one in Bombay, by the Indian scholar S.P. Pandit, and others in Europe in German and French. This play's most recent English translation, by the Columbia University academic David Gitomer, appeared in 1984.[v]

Within India, the literary standing of Kalidasa has always been high. This is evident from the words of many eminent commentators who lived at different times and places in the country. To give some idea of this, here are three comments: by the poet Bana, from the seventh-century empire of Harsha in the north, the writer Appaya Dikshita from the fourteenth-century Vijayanagara empire in the south, and the famous Rabindranath Tagore from twentieth-century modern India, who needs no introduction. All wrote verses in praise of Kalidasa, the first two in Sanskrit, and the last in Bangla. Their earlier published translations are given here to provide today's reader with a flavour of the sentiments that Kalidasa's work has inspired over many centuries at different places in his own land.[vi]

> Who would not delighted be
> when Kalidasa's well said words,
> came forth, charming with sweet scents,
> like flower buds in nectar soaked?

—Bana

> In the count of ancient poets
> Kalidasa does at the first place stay,
> for the lack of one comparable,
> the next is nameless to this day.

—Appaya Diksita

> Ah, supreme poet, that first, hallowed day
> Of Asadh on which, in some unknown year, you wrote
> Your Meghaduta! Your stanzas are themselves
> Like dark layered sonorous clouds, heaping the misery
> Of separated lovers throughout the world
> Into thunderous music.

—Rabindranath Tagore[vii]

*

One may now turn to the play here translated. It begins with dramatic circumstances: of the first contact between the royal hero and the heroine nymph with her companions, and of her rescue from a demon by him. This leads to their initial mutual attraction, later discussed between the king and his friend, the royal jester, who has also been approached in this matter by the former's consort, the queen. The two friends go to a garden where both the heroine and the queen also appear separately. The former and the hero talk of their feelings for each other, but she is called back to heaven on urgent summons. The hero also tells his wife about the heroine and seeks her forgiveness, but she too leaves the scene. All this is in the first two acts. In the third act, these inter-personal contacts continue. The queen accepts her husband's relationship with the heroine, who is then present but invisible. On the queen's departure, the hero and heroine again confirm their mutual love.

The fourth act of this Kalidasa play is considered a musical drama on its own. The hero and the heroine are on a pleasure trip. There she is enraged by his staring at another woman. Ignoring his entreaties, she enters a forbidden grove and is there transformed into a creeper vine. Mad in despair, the hero wanders in the forest, in search of his beloved, singing, dancing and tearfully asking animals and plants about her. Eventually he finds a magical gem that brings her back in person to their loving reunion. The final act is set later in time. It appears that the now long-time lovers had a son whom the nymph had hidden since birth from the father to avoid a heavenly curse. The son, Ayush, now appears in a yet another drama. The family is reunited and a celestial sage comes to announce the curse's withdrawal and a happy end.

*

The foregoing is for the modern reader, unfamiliar with this play. It can hopefully be further savoured with a dip into this translation. For those interested in the play's scholarly consideration and critical understanding, there are many detailed serious works, some mentioned in the notes that follow. But, for a feel and flavour of this work as a whole, here are some episodes of Kalidasa's own creation that the interested reader may see in the text of the present translation.

The first is doubtless that from Act Four, in which the hero sings and dances in the forest as he searches for the heroine. This is accompanied by moving songs and recitations by unnamed artists offstage, not in courtly Sanskrit but in colloquial dialects of Prakrit and Apabhramsa that convey their own emotional beauty. The whole comprises a moving musical soliloquy and dialogue exceptional to this play.

Then there are some vivid instances introduced by Kalidasa within the dramatic action. One is about finding the Gem of Reunion that leads the hero to embrace a particular creeper vine that then turns into his beloved, the heroine.

The gem is later stolen by a vulture that is shot down by their son, and results in the family's reunion.

Others are some glimpses of the background to Urvashi's relations with Pururavas. How she was cursed to leave heaven when she uttered by mistake her lover's name while dancing before the king of the gods, and how that curse was later modified by a command for her return to heaven when the hero first saw her child by him. She was also finally accepted by her lover's spouse, the queen, leading to her son being asked to first greet his senior mother.

A look at the interaction mentioned in the *Rig Veda* hymn gives some idea of how this play's story evolved over the millennia. In the words of the modern scholar, David Gitomer, the vedic hymn alternates at its end between 'the pathetic pleas of Pururavas with Urvashi's rather cold remembrance of their affair and adamant refusal' and her warning to him that 'there can be no friendship with women: their hearts are like the hearts of jackals'.[viii] The motif of a curse on Urvashi only appeared in later versions of the tale. Kalidasa retained it, though his hero's loving heart is still the same throughout. But in his play Urvashi is depicted as a person with human compassion rather than divine disdain.

There is a pertinent comment on the foregoing by the distinguished scholar H.D. Velankar, who edited this play for the critical edition undertaken by India's official literary institution, Sahitya Akademi. In his words, 'Kalidasa by his superb art turned the self-conscious, imperious and hard-hearted Urvashi of Vedic literature', into a faithful, deeply loving consort of the king who too reciprocated, 'her love with a single minded devotion'.[ix]

In his editor's introduction, Velankar also commented at length on the non-Sanskrit dialogue that dominates Act Four of the play. In a detailed scholarly overview he distinguished between the usage of the Sanskrit-linked dialects Apabhramsa and Prakrit in it, respectively by the king and the offstage singers, during the former's search for his beloved. While this analysis may be of relevance for scholarly study, in another matter of a more general interest he also dwelt on the significance of this play's title to its overall theme.

In earlier times, the title *Vikramorvashiyam* appears to have been understood as referring just to the couple, that is the hero and the heroine. The latter's name in it is indeed clear in the title. But the name preceding it was considered as a reference to the hero in terms of the title 'Vikramaditya' held by the then Gupta king, whose patronage was perhaps being sought by the playwright. Velankar suggested that the prefix 'Vikrama' in the play's title simply indicates the literal meaning of 'valour', which was displayed by Pururavas in his pursuit of Urvashi. This view now seems accepted, and the play's title, as given in the last English translation by Gitomer is 'Urvashi Won by Valour'.[x] Another meaning is 'valour in a quest'. This is reflected in the title of the present translation.

*

This new translation is based on the original Velankar text, authorized and published by the Sahitya Akademi in 1961. Also consulted was an earlier but still well-known text, edited and translated with a Sanskrit commentary, by M.R. Kale in 1889 and last reprinted in 1967. This excluded the then controversial but now accepted non-Sanskrit portions in Act Four, but is useful for the rest of the text.[xi] Here it may be added that most Sanskrit dramas have non-Sanskrit dialogue which was traditional for roles of women and common folk, but in this play it has a special significance in relation to the king's own despondent condition.

As with my previous Penguin translations of Kalidasa,[xii] this too attempts to convey something of the original's literary spirit and tone in a direct retelling of the original Sanskrit. The scenes and moods, the characters and dialogues created in this play by Kalidasa are dramatic and lively, but also sensitive and colourful. I have tried to transmit them from the original in contemporary language. It was a wonderful experience, but needed much effort.

In conclusion, I thank Penguin Random House India for the opportunity to translate this play, the last of the seven Kalidasa works that will complete their special series on the great poet-dramatist. It was also a pleasure for me, especially after doing his *Raghuvamsam* and *Ritusaharam* for them in the past years. I am grateful to Ambar Sahil Chatterjee, with whom this work was initiated, and to Ananya Bhatia and Tarini Uppal who brought it to completion. My thanks also to the New Delhi libraries of Sahitya Akademi and India International Centre for help with reference material. But I have no words for expressing my deepest gratitude to my wife, Priti, whose love, care and support in this work enabled it being done at a trying time for me. It is now dedicated to our dear and always helpful son, Vikram, who shares both the name in the prefix of this play's title, as well as the qualities of prowess and valour that it signifies.

A.N.D.H.
New Delhi
March 2021

VIKRAMORVASHIYAM

List of Cast

In Order of Appearance

(Some characters appear in several acts, but are named here only at first appearance.)

Act One

Stage Manager:	*Sutradhara* in Sanskrit. Director of the play and the players
Assistant:	Named Marisha, who helps the stage manager
Three Nymphs:	Rambha, Menaka, Sahajanya. Celestial nymphs, apsaras in Sanskrit.
King:	Pururavas, ruler of Pratishthana, and the hero
Charioteer:	Drives the king's chariot
Chitralekha:	Celestial nymph, companion of Urvashi

Urvashi:	Celestial nymph and the heroine
Chitraratha:	Chief of heavenly singers

Act Two

Jester:	A brahmin named Manavaka, the king's companion and friend
Nipunika:	Personal maid of Queen Aushinari, the king's wife
Queen:	Aushinari, daughter of the king of Kashi and chief wife of Pururavas

Act Three

Two Pupils:	Of Bharata, patron sage of drama. Named Pallava and Galava, not described individually
Chamberlain:	Of King Pururavas. Named Latavya, not described individually
Maid:	Of the queen, not described individually
Queen's Retinue:	Other maidservants, not described individually

Act Five

King's Retinue:	Chamberlain, a huntress, a Greek woman bow-bearer and others

Hermit Woman:	From the hermitage of sage Chyavana, named Satyavati and guardian of Urvashi's son
Boy:	Prince Ayush, son of Urvashi from the king
Narada:	A divine sage from heaven, and messenger from the king of gods.

Offstage Voices

Act One:	(1) Recitation of the Benediction
	(2) A cry for help
Act Two:	Divine messenger summoning Urvashi to heaven
Act Four:	(1) Singers offstage as the king searches for Urvashi in the forest
	(2) Voice advising the king about the Gem of Reunion
Act Five:	(1) Maid servant who carried the Gem of Reunion stolen by a vulture
	(2) Two bards singing offstage at the end

Act One

Benediction

Voice Offstage:

The scriptures have described him
as that entity unique
which pervades both worlds.
To him alone applies the word
Ishvara, ruler supreme.
Those who are seeking salvation,
while controlling all their senses,
look for him within themselves.
And he is easily attainable
through discipline and devotion.
May Sthanu,[i] the eternal Shiva
Give to you the highest bliss. (1)

End of Benediction

(*Enter Stage Manager.*)

Stage Manager (*looking behind*): Marisha, come here!

Assistant (*entering*): Here I am, sir.

Stage Manager: Marisha, this noble audience has often witnessed the works of earlier dramatists. Today I will stage before them a new play, *Vikramorvashiyam*. Tell all actors to be careful with their parts.

Assistant: As you command, sir.

(*Exits.*)

Stage Manager: Now, I would like to request all the honoured people here:

> Either with kindness for your servants,
> or with respect for a hero great,
> please follow with minds attentive
> now, this work by Kalidasa. (2)

Voice Offstage: Help! Help!

Stage Manager (*listening*): Oh, what is this? As I was making my request, there is a sound of distress from the sky.

It is like the shriek of an osprey bird. (*Thinks.*) Well, I know what it is:

> A nymph celestial, with a name
> that denotes birth from the thigh[ii]
> of a sage who was friendly to men,
> had gone to serve Kailasa's lord,
> and while returning did get seized,
> midway, by a demon foe.
> And her nymph companions are
> now weeping so pitifully. (3)

(*Exits.*)

(*Enter the nymphs.*)

Nymphs: Help! O help, some friend of the gods, one who can move in the sky!

(*The back-curtain is pulled aside. Enter the king on a chariot with the charioteer.*)

King: Stop! Stop your weeping! I am Pururavas, on my way back after saluting the Sun. Come, tell me, with what do you ladies need help?

Rambha: From an attack by a demon!

King: But what has he done to you?

Menaka: Listen, great king. It is our dear friend Urvashi. An ornament of heaven, her beauty shames the goddess Shri,[iii] who is so proud of her own. She is also the delicate weapon used by the great god Indra, when he is troubled by some special saintly austerity. As we were returning from Kubera's[iv] palace, she and her friend Chitralekha were seized midway by a demon and taken away.

King: In which direction did that villain go? Are you aware?

Sahajanya: It was to the north-east.

King: Then stop worrying. I will go and try to get her back.

Nymphs: This is indeed as it should be, with one born in the Moon's dynasty![v]

King: Where will you ladies wait for me?

Nymphs: At the golden peaked mountain, Hemakuta.[vi]

King: Charioteer, urge the horses for a quick rush to the north-eastern quarter.

Charioteer: As you command, long-living lord. (*Does as ordered.*)

King (*observing the chariot's speed*): Well done! Well done! With such a fast chariot, I can overtake even the eagle Garuda though he may have started earlier. What to say of the demon that has offended Indra.

> And clouds before the chariot's path
> are now scattered just like dust,
> and the whirling wheels appear
> to have new spokes amidst the old,
> the plumes upon the heads of horses
> are still as if in a picture,
> and the flag looks flat, not fluttering,
> such is the wind's velocity.   (4)

(*Exit the king, chariot and charioteer.*)

Rambha: Friends, let us also go to the place agreed upon.

(*After enacting their descent on the mountain, all nymphs stand there.*)

Rambha: Will the saintly king be able to remove that painful splinter from our hearts?

Menaka: You should not doubt him. When faced with aggression, even great Indra invites him with utmost respect from the earth, to lead the army to victory.

Rambha: May he always be victorious!

Sahajanya (*after a momentary pause*): Cheer up, friends. Cheer up! There is the king's moon-bestowed chariot with a leaping deer on its banner! And he is not coming back without success!

(*All nymphs look upwards as the king returns in the chariot. In it is Urvashi, her eyes closed in fear and hand held by Chitralekha.*)

Chitralekha: Take heart, dear friend. Cheer up!

King: Have courage, O beauty! Have courage:

> Gone, shy one, is the terror caused
> by that demon, foe of the gods;
> the power of the thunder-bolt wielder[vii]
> protects all the three worlds.
> O lotus-eyed one, open your eyes,
> like a lotus blooms at dawn.   (5)

Chitralekha: Alas! Her breath is the only sign of life in her. Even now, she hasn't regained consciousness.

King: She has been terribly frightened—

> The fear that is within her heart
> has not yet stopped its trembling:

see, it is clear from the sandal paste
between her heaving breasts. (6)

Chitralekha: This is unlike a nymph. Compose yourself, my
friend.

(*Urvashi revives.*)

King: Ah, your friend is back to normal!

It seems that she is free of stupor,
like the light released from darkness,
as the moon appears;
or, a sacrificial fire's flame
piercing through the smoke at night;
or the muddied river Ganga,
getting back its glow. (7)

Chitralekha: Friend, be at ease. The demon who defied the
gods has been defeated.

Urvashi (*opening her eyes*): Was it by the power shown by the
great god Indra?

Chitralekha: Not by the great Indra! But by this saintly king
whose prowess is no less!

Urvashi (*to herself, after seeing the king*): The demon has done me a favour.

King (*to himself, after seeing Urvashi back to normal*): I now understand why all the nymphs, who were sent to seduce the sage Narayana, were embarrassed on seeing what emerged from his thigh. But how could a sage create her?[viii]

> Indeed the moon, all creatures' lord,
> must have given her this glow,
> or Madana, the god of love,
> whose special *rasa*[ix] is erotic,
> or the season that brings flowers:
> for how could an ancient sage,
> his person with scriptures rigid,
> and interest in pleasures gone,
> create such an enchantress? (8)

Urvashi: Friend, where are our other comrades?

Chitralekha: This great king would know. He freed us from fear.

King (*looking at Urvashi*): They were in a lot of gloom. Look, my lady,

> One who has seen you only once,
> upon his path, O beauty,

and his eyes are fixed on you:
for you, he too would anxious be,
what to say of the deep affection
that your friends do have for you.   (9)

Urvashi (*to herself*): His words are indeed noble. But hardly surprising, for nectar does flow from the moon. (*Aloud.*) That is why my heart does yearn for them!

King (*pointing with his hand*):

Fair one, your friends who had proceeded
to the golden mountain, will now see
the radiance your face displays,
like the moon when an eclipse is over.   (10)

Chitralekha: Friend, look!

Urvashi (*with a sidelong look at the king*): Just a look drives away the pain from my eyes!

Chitralekha (*knowingly*): At whom?

Urvashi: At all these friends.

Rambha (*joyfully*): Here is that royal sage! With Urvashi and Chitralekha! Like the moon, he has arrived with starry constellations.

Menaka: Both our wishes are fulfilled. Our friends are back! And, the great king is unhurt!

Sahajanya: Friend, you are right. We all know how difficult it is to defeat demons.

(*All nymphs approach the king.*)

King: Charioteer, stop. I will get down.

Charioteer: As you command, noble one.

(*Acts as ordered.*)

King (*to himself, miming the sense of a jolt*): This rough descent gave me a good result.

> With the jolting of this chariot,
> my shoulder touched her rounded hips,
> and with a thrill my hair did bristle,
> sprouted by the god of love. (11)

Urvashi (*bashfully*): Friend, shift a bit.

Chitralekha (*with a smile*): I can't!

Rambha: So, let us approach the royal sage.

(*All nymphs approach the king.*)

King: Charioteer, halt the chariot,

> So that this most eager beauty
> may now embrace her friends,
> like the glory that is spring
> embellishes the forest vines. (12)

Nymphs: Congratulations for your victory, great king.

King: And to you too, ladies, on meeting your friend.

(*Urvashi alights from the chariot, holding Chitralekha's hand.*)

Urvashi: Friends, embrace me! Tightly! Indeed I had no hope of seeing you all again.

(*The friends hug her.*)

Rambha: Great king, may you protect this earth in every way for hundreds of ages.

Charioteer: Noble sir, there is a strong sound of a chariot at speed from the East.

And there is someone mounted on it,
with arm bands of beaten gold.
It descends on this mountain peak,
like a cloud streaked with lightning.   (13)

Nymphs: Oh! Here is Chitraratha!

(*Enter Chitraratha.*)

Chitraratha (*standing before the king*): Congratulations, sir. Your fame multiplies with your valour—sufficient even to assist the great Indra.

King: Oh! The chief of heavenly singers! (*Getting down from his chariot.*) Welcome, dear friend.

(*They clasp each other's hands.*)

Chitraratha: Great Indra heard from Narada that Urvashi had been kidnapped by the demon Keshin. He then ordered the army of celestial singers to get her back. On the way, we heard from the bards about your victory, and have come here to you. She must salute Indra, together with you and me. For you have indeed done what he wanted, sir. Look,

Long ago did the sage Narayana
present her to the king of heaven,

and now she has been rescued
by you from the demon's hands.   (14)

King: No! It is not so!

It is indeed by the power of
the wielder of the thunderbolt,
that his allies defeat the foe:
from his mountain cave, even the echo
of a lion's roar can terrify elephants.   (15)

Chitraratha: This is quite well said. Modesty does indeed
ornament valour.

King: This is no time for me to visit Indra, the lord of a hundred
sacrifices. You should yourself take this lady to meet him.

Chitraratha: As you wish, sir. Ladies, this way.

(*The nymphs mime to leave.*)

Urvashi: Friend Chitralekha, though this saintly king did save
me, I cannot say good-bye to him. So, please be my mouthpiece.

Chitralekha (*approaching the king*): Great king, Urvashi says
she wants to express her gratitude to you and, as for a dear
friend, to carry your fame to great Indra's realm.

King: Do go, till we meet each other again.

(*The nymphs mime mounting to the sky, together with the celestial singers.*)

Uravashi (*miming great reluctance*): Alas! My string of pearls has been caught in the vine of a creeper plant. Chitralekha, please set it free.

Chitralekha (*with a smile*): It is stuck hard, and is difficult to disentangle. But I will try to do it.

Urvashi: Remember your words!

King (*to himself*):

> Creeper, to me your deed is dear,
> it delays for a while her going,
> and her side-long glance at me
> as she turns away her face, I see.   (16)

Charioteer: Noble lord,

> Having hurled into the sea
> the demon who had great Indra wronged,
> your wind-like arrow has again

come back to its quiver now,
like a serpent to its burrow. (17)

King: Then, bring back the chariot so that I may mount it.

(*The charioteer does so and the king mounts the chariot. Urvashi gazes at him and sighs as she exits with her friend Chitralekha.*)

King (*looking towards where Urvashi has gone*): Alas! My desires did look for something hard to attain!

As she flies to her father, the sky,
this divine damsel has torn
the heart out from my body,
like the mate of a royal swan
pulls a stalk from a lotus bloom. (18)

(*Exit all.*)

End of Act One

Act Two

(*Enter the royal jester.*)

Jester: Oh! Oh! Oh! I am bursting with the king's secret inside me! Like the brahmin invited to a feast with the grub! But, when surrounded by people, I may not be able to control my tongue. So, till my royal comrade gets up from his seat of work, I will stay in this hall downstairs, where few people come.

(*Walks about the stage. Then, enter a maidservant.*)

Maidservant: I am commanded by the queen, daughter of the king of Kashi. 'Nipunika,' she ordered, 'our lord's mind seems lost since he returned after saluting the Sun. Find out the cause of his condition from his dear friend, the jester Manavaka.' Now, how can I get to that brotherly brahmin? But a secret can stay within him no longer than a drop of water on the tip of a twig. So, I will look for him.

(*Wanders about and sees him.*) Oh, there is the noble Manavaka, sitting still, like a monkey in a picture. I will go to him. Noble sir, my salutations.

Jester: Greetings, lady! (*To himself.*) This wicked maid will leave me only after getting the king's secret out of my heart! (*To her.*) Nipunika, how is it that you come here, leaving your practice of music aside?

Nipunika: The queen has sent me to you, sir.

Jester: What has the lady commanded?

Nipunika: The queen says that you have always been on her side, and never ignored any uncalled for pain that she may suffer.

Jester: Nipunika, what has my comrade the king done against the lady?

Nipunika: The queen was addressed by her lord with the name of another woman, for whom he is now full of longing.

Jester (*to himself*): What? He has himself let out that secret? Then why should I suffer and hold back my tongue? (*To the maid.*) Was our lady addressed as Urvashi? His seeing that woman has maddened our lord. And that affects not only the queen, but even me since he has given up his usual enjoyments.

Nipunika (*to herself*): I have found out the secret of our master! (*To the jester.*) Sir, what shall I tell the queen?

Jester: Nipunika. Tell our lady that I will try to turn my comrade away from this mirage. Then I will inform her myself.

Nipunika: As you command, sir. (*Exits.*)

Bard (*offstage*): Victory, O King!

> We know that your efforts and your rights
> do compare with those of the Sun:
> in removing from the world
> nature's darkness, and of people.
> The Sun stops for a moment in the sky
> as the master of all stars;
> and you too keep a sixth of the day
> for doing as you please. (1)

Jester (*listening*): My comrade has risen from his seat, and comes this way. I will go to his side. (*Exits.*)

(*Enter the king, filled with longing, and the jester.*)

King:

> From the time since she was seen
> that beauty divine has entered my heart.
> It was pierced and split wide open
> by an arrow of the god of love. (2)

Jester (*to himself*): Indeed. Ever since then has that poor daughter of the king of Kashi been miserable.

King: Has my secret stayed safe with you?

Jester (*sadly, to himself*): That servant maid deceived me! Otherwise my comrade would not ask this.

King: Why are you silent?

Jester: Sir. I don't give sudden answers. Even to you. Thus is my tongue kept under control.

King: Alright. But then, how should I divert myself?

Jester: Let's go to the kitchen.

King: Why there?

Jester: One's longings can be relieved there. By looking at the procurement, and then at the preparation, of all the five types of food.

King: Well, you would enjoy the presence of all that you crave for. But how will that please me, who seeks something so hard to get?

Jester: Sir, there you would be in the lady Urvashi's range of sight!

King: Then what?

Jester: Then she may not be so hard to get!

King: You are just taking my side.

Jester: This makes me more curious. Is she as incomparable in beauty, as I am in ugliness?

King: Manavaka, it is impossible to describe her limb by limb. So, here is a summary. Listen.

Jester: I am all attention.

King:

> An ornament of ornaments,
> an embellishment to all decoration,
> her form cannot be compared, friend,
> nor is any thing worth comparison. (3)

Jester: So, you seek a divine nectar, sir, and have indeed taken the vow of a *chataka* bird.[i]

King: Friend, for a mind filled with longing, there is no refuge except in solitude. So, lead the way to some pleasure-garden.

Jester (*to himself*): What way? (*Aloud.*) This way, sir, this way! (*Moving around.*) Here is the pleasure-garden, sir, and it has inspired the southern breeze to greet you on arrival.

King (*looking around*): That's a good gesture by the breeze. It,

> Sprinkles nectar drops upon
> the tender, sweet, spring creeper,
> and makes the vine of jasmine dance,
> uniting courtesy and desire,
> like a person deep in love. (4)

Jester: May your devotion be similar. There is the pleasure-garden's gate. Do enter, sir.

King: After you.

(*Both mime entering.*)

King (*looking ahead*): Friend, I was wrong in thinking that my problems would be solved by coming here:

I came to this garden swiftly
to cool the fire within,
but it is like swimming against
a current carrying one away. (5)

Jester: How so?

King: To start is difficult, then hard to stop—

First, my heart was indeed pierced
by the five arrows of Kama,
then again by this scented breeze
wafting through a mango grove,
brushing off its withered leaves
and revealing fresh new buds. (6)

Jester: Stop lamenting! Kama will himself help you to get what you want.

King: Well, I accept the words of a brahmin!

(*Both walk around.*)

Jester: Sir, look at the beauty of this pleasure-garden. It announces the arrival of spring!

King: I see that at every step—

Here are blooms of the amaranth,
dark on either side, but with tips
pale like a woman's finger nail;
there stands the young ashoka sapling,
about to open scarlet blossoms;
and new buds on the mango tree
seem covered with their pollen dust;
midst the bud and the flower, friend,
spreads the splendour of the spring.   (7)

Jester: Here is a bower of vines with pearl like blooms. And within it is a marble bench, scattered with flowers dropped by bumblebees. Grace it, sir. It seems to have been made for you.

King: As you say.

(*Both sit down.*)

Jester: Well, sir, you are seated here comfortably. Focus your eyes on those delicate creepers, to divest yourself of the longing for Urvashi.

King (*with a sigh*):

My eyes cannot now be attracted
to this garden's tender shoots and vines:

friend, they are already fixed upon
gazing at her graceful beauty. (8)

So, think of a way, by which this, my desire, can be fulfilled.

Jester (*laughing*): The thunderbolt of the great Indra, looking for Ahalya!ⁱⁱ And I, helping you to find Urvashi! Well, we both are mad!

King: Indeed it is a great affection, and it does show the way.

Jester: I am thinking of one. But please don't disturb my thoughts again with lamentation. (*Acts immersed in thought.*)

King (*to himself, as if seeing an omen*):

She is not easy to attain,
that girl with a face like the moon,
but there is a sign from the god of love
for fulfilment of my longing,
and my heart does suddenly
experience a sense of calm. (9)

(*Stands up hopefully. Then enter Urvashi and Chitralekha, by a chariot from the sky.*)

Chitralekha: Friend, where is this chariot going, for some reason unknown?

Urvashi: Why do you ask now? On the Golden Mountain peak too, we had been held up for a moment by something caught in that bush of vines.

Chitralekha: What? Are you going to that saintly king, to Pururavas?

Urvashi: Well, this is my shameless way!

Chitralekha: And what, friend, takes you on that way?

Urvashi: My heart.

Chitralekha: For me, that is not an answer.

Urvashi: Then tell me, friend, of a way to go, free of obstacles.

Chitralekha: Be calm, friend. Didn't the guru of the gods teach us how to keep our hair in a knot called Aparajita,[iii] so that demons could not harm us?

Urvashi: Friend, I remember it all.

(*They descend on the sages' path.*)

Chitralekha: Here we are. At the saintly king's palace, that gazes at its own reflection in the sacred waters where the rivers

Ganga and Yamuna meet. It is the crest-jewel of Pratishthan, his capital.

Urvashi (*gazing*): It should indeed be called a new heaven. But, where could he be? That protector of the fallen.

Chitralekha: We will find out after getting down in that pleasure-garden, another Nandana, the park of paradise.

(*Both come down.*)

Chitralekha (*delighted at seeing the king*): There he is, friend, like the moon awaiting its moonlight, as it rises.

Urvashi (*observing him*): Friend, that great king's glory looks even more delightful than when I saw him first.

Chitralekha: This is natural. Come, let us get closer.

Urvashi: I will make myself invisible, and stand beside him. Then listen to what he is saying to some friend with no one else around.

Chitralekha: As you like. (*Both mime becoming invisible.*)

Jester: Sir, I have thought of a way for you to unite with your beloved. So, hear my reply.

(*The king stays silent.*)

Urvashi: Who could that woman be? She whom he seeks and who thinks just of herself?

Chitralekha: Why are you acting like a human?

Urvashi: Because I am suddenly afraid to find this out through my own powers.

Jester: I now speak of a method for meeting her, one that I have thought of.

King: Say it.

Jester: Go to sleep, sir, and meet her in a dream. Or, make a portrait of lady Urvashi, and look at it.

Urvashi (*excited*): Be reassured, my poor heart, be reassured!

King: Neither of these methods will work—

> This heart is ever being pierced
> by the arrows of the god of love,
> how can I then fall asleep,
> to meet her in a dream?
> As for the portrait of my beloved,

it would never be completed,
for as I draw that lovely picture, friend,
my eyes will always fill with tears. (10)

Chitralekha: Did you hear that?

Urvashi: I did. But it is not enough for my heart.

Jester (*speaking to the king*): That is all I that I can think of.

King (*with a sigh*):

She does not know the torture
my heart does suffer;
or her powers reveal it,
but my love she ignores.
May the god with five arrows,
who first rendered it fruitless,
make my thirst for uniting
with that woman now succeed. (11)

Chitralekha: Did you hear that?

Urvashi: Oh dear! Oh dear, thus does he think of me! But I am unable to stand before him and respond. So I will use my powers and send him a reply written on birch-bark.

Chitralekha: I agree.

(*Urvashi mimes writing a message.*)

Jester: Oh! Oh! What has fallen before me? It looks like the cast-off skin of a snake.

King (*looking*): It is something written on a birch-bark.

Jester: Indeed! It may be something written and dropped by an invisible Urvashi, after hearing your words, and to convey her own love for you.

King: There is no limit to wishing. (*Takes and reads it with joy.*) Friend, your guess was a good one.

Jester: And I too would like to hear what is written there.

Urvashi: Great! Sir, you are a gentleman.

King: Listen. (*Reads out.*)

> Lord, perhaps you do not know
> how much I am in love with you:
> my body gets so hot with it
> that it finds no peace in lying

on a bed of coral jasmine blooms
cooled by the heavenly garden's breeze. (12)

Urvashi: What indeed will he now say?

Chitralekha: It has already been said by the thrill on his limbs, like that on lotus stems.

Jester: Sir, you have been reassured! For me, it is like an offer of food when one is famished.

King: Just reassured? Why say only that?

The delicate meaning of those words
in the message from my darling
does display comparable love.
Her glances that intoxicate
and the feelings on my face,
friend, they are already together. (13)

Urvashi: This is our love! It is equally shared!

King: Hold it, comrade. It is written in my beloved's own hand. The sweat from my fingers may smudge the letters.

Jester (*taking it*): Sir, the lady Urvashi has manifested the blossoming of your desire. Will she now deny you its fruit?

Urvashi: My heart is too timid to approach him, friend. So, will you go to the king and say what I would like?

Chitralekha: So be it. (*Discards invisibility and approaches the king.*) Victory to you, victory, great king.

King (*joyfully*): Welcome, blessed lady.

> But, in the absence of your friend,
> you cannot delight me thus,
> like the river Yamuna with no Ganga,
> earlier seen at their confluence. (14)

Chitralekha: Well, one first sees the row of clouds, and only then the flash of lightning!

Jester (*aside*): What is this? Not Urvashi, but only her close friend?

Chitralekha: Urvashi salutes you, great king, and makes a request.

King: What does she command?

Chitralekha: 'When I was in trouble caused by an enemy of the gods,' she says, 'the great king was my sole refuge. But after seeing the king, I am now tightly bound by desire, and also need his compassion.'

King: Fair one,

> You describe that lovely beauty
> as being love-sick, but do not see
> the pain of Pururavas for her.
> Mutual is our love, one for the other:
> two irons that are burning hot,
> deserve to be welded together. (15)

Chitralekha (*approaching Urvashi*): Come, my friend. Seeing that the god of love has been even more pitiless with your lover, I am now his messenger.

Urvashi (*discarding her invisibility*): So, you have quickly abandoned me?

Chitralekha (*with a smile*): In a moment will I know who has abandoned whom! Meanwhile, behave yourself.

Urvashi (*bashfully*): Victory, victory great king!

King: O Beauty!

Victory is indeed mine
to whom you utter this word,
never addressed to any man,
except that god of thousand eyes.[iv]   (16)

(*He takes her hand and seats her.*)

Jester: Lady, why no salute for this brahmin, a good friend of the king?

(*Urvashi smiles and salutes him.*)

Jester: All the best, lady!

(*There is a voice from back stage.*)

Divine Messenger: Chitralekha, hurry up with Urvashi:

Our master wishes to see today,
together with the guardian gods,
that performance, gorgeously
suffused with all the rasas eight,
that which has been taught to her
by Bharata, the saintly sage.   (17)

(*All listen. Urvashi mimes sadness.*)

Chitralekha: You heard the divine messenger's words? Now take leave of the king.

Urvashi: I don't have the words.

Chitralekha: Great king, she is a vassal of someone else. She does not want to offend the gods, if you permit.

King (*in words carefully chosen*): I cannot oppose her lord's command. But remember the being you leave behind here.

(*Displaying pain at separation, Urvashi exits with her friend.*)

King (*with a sigh*): Friend, my eyes now seem useless.

Jester (*wishing to show the birch-bark*): Here it is, but . . . (*To himself.*) Alas! Alas! I was wonderstruck at seeing Urvashi, and have carelessly dropped that birch-bark.

King: What do you want to say?

Jester: Do not despair, sir. Urvashi is firmly attached to you. Her love will not slacken.

King: I too feel that in my heart. As she departed,

Her sighs and the trembling of her breasts
did make it clear that she was not
the mistress of her body, for
her heart she has given to me.   (18)

Jester (*to himself*): My heart trembles too, as the lord will now ask for that birch-bark letter.

King: Now, what can divert my eyes? (*Remembering.*) Oh, bring me that birch-bark letter.

Jester (*miming despair*): Oh dear, it is not here. Perhaps it went with Urvashi. (*Mimes a search.*)

(*Enter the queen, daughter of the king of Kashi, with her entourage.*)

Queen: Nipunika, did you speak the truth in saying that you saw our lord entering this grove with his friend, the noble Manavaka?

Nipunika: Have I ever said anything else to my lady?

Queen: Then I will hide behind that creeper vine and privately listen to their talk and find out if what you told me was true.

Nipunika: As you wish, my lady.

Queen (*walks around*): What is that, O Nipunika? It looks an old rag, blown here by the southern breeze.

Nipunika: It is a piece of birch-bark with some letters written on one side. Oh! It is now caught in my lady's anklet. What now? Shall we read it?

Queen: Read it to yourself first. If it is alright, I will then listen to it.

Nipunika (*does so*): It seems something scandalous, my lady. I think a poem by Urvashi addressed to our lord. It has come into our hands because of Manavaka's carelessness.

Queen: Then I would like to know what it says.

(*Nipunika reads out the verse earlier read by the king.*)

Queen: Well, I will meet that nymph's lover with this very gift.

(*Turns towards the bower with her attendants.*)

Jester: Friend, what is that, fluttering in the air by the hillside near the pleasure garden?

King (*rising*): O honoured southern breeze, loved by spring:

For its fragrance, takes away
the scented pollen of spring flowers,
but why, for nothing, must you take
what my love wrote with her own hand.
You please your own dear Anjana,^v
and know how a lover is sustained
by such things to divert the mind.   (19)

Nipunika: My lady, here is the very same letter being searched for.

Queen: I see.

Jester: Oh, I was deceived by a peacock's tail feather that looked like a withered *kesara,* the saffron flower.

King: And I am now finished!

Queen (*approaching him*): Don't worry, my lord. Here is that birch-bark.

King (*in confusion*): Oh, it is the queen. Welcome, my lady.

Jester (*aside*): Unwelcome, now!

King (*separately to the Jester*): Friend, what should be done now?

Jester: What can a thief say when caught with his plunder?

King (*aside*): Fool, this is no time for a joke. (*Aloud.*) My lady, it is not for this that I was searching. It was for an official letter that our search had been undertaken.

Queen: But it was used for hiding someone's own good luck!

Jester: My lady, he might be given a quick dinner to alleviate his pique!

Queen: Nipunika, how nicely does this brahmin defend his friend!

Jester: Indeed, my lady. All can be pleased with a good meal.

King: Fool, you are doing your best to prove me guilty.

Queen: My lord, it is not your fault. I alone am guilty in standing before you and displaying contrariness. So, I will go away. (*Mimes anger and starts to leave.*)

King:

> Please give up your anger
> it is I who am guilty:
> when one who is served, is enraged,
> how can the servant be free of guilt? (20)

(*Falls at her feet.*)

Queen (*to herself*): I can accept contrition, for my heart is not small. But I am afraid that charity may lead to regret.

(*Steps away from the king and exits with her retinue.*)

Jester: The queen was like a river in the rainy season. But she has gone. So, get up.

King (*getting up*): That was not wrong. Look,

> A lover's sweet words of contrition,
> even a hundred, cannot enter
> the hearts of women, in this condition.
> They look artificial, like a fake gemstone.   (21)

Jester: Anyway it is convenient, sir. Indeed, one cannot stare at a lamp light if the eyes are hurting.

King: It is not like that. Even though my heart is set on Urvashi, I have great respect for the queen. But falling at her feet has had no effect, and so I have to rely on patience.

Jester: Sir, you can be patient. But the life of this hungry brahmin depends on you. It is time for a bath and dinner.

King: Well,

> Troubled by heat, the peacock sits
> by waters cool beneath a tree;
> piercing through a flower bud
> inside it hides itself the bee;
> abandoning lake waters hot,
> ducks rest near lotuses by the shore;
> but the tired parrot in a cage
> at a rest house, begs for water more.   (22)

(*Exit all.*)

End of Act Two

Act Three

(*Enter two disciples of the sage Bharata.*)[i]

First: Friend Pallava, our teacher had you carry his stool when he went to great Indra's palace. I was kept back to guard the sacred fire. So, I ask you. Was the divine assembly pleased by the performance of that play, put on by our guru?

Second: I don't know if they were pleased. That play had been composed by Saraswati, the goddess of speech. It was *Lakshmi Svayamvara*, that is, 'Lakshmi's Choice of a Bridegroom'. Urvashi was totally engrossed in its dramatic moods.

First: From your words it seems there was some fault.

Second: Yes. Urvashi seemed agitated, and mispronounced some of her words.

First: How?

Second: She played the role of Lakshmi. Menaka, who acted as Varuni, asked her: 'Friend, the gods who guard the three worlds are gathered here along with Keshava. Who among them attracts your feelings of love?'[ii]

First: And then?

Second: Then she should have said 'Purushottama', another name of the god Keshava or Vishnu. But the name that she uttered was 'Pururavas'!

First: Well, one's senses conform to one's destiny. Didn't the guru get angry with her?

Second: Our guru cursed her. But the great Indra was sympathetic.

First: How was that?

First: Our guru's curse was: 'As you transgressed my teaching, you will lose your place in heaven.' But when Indra, the smasher of citadels, noticed Urvashi's face downcast with shame, he said to her: 'That saintly king, to whom you are attracted, has helped me in battle, and I owe him some favour. So, stay with him as he desires, till he sees your offspring from him.'

First: That was like the great Indra, who knows the hearts of others.

Second (*gazing at the sun*): In the course of our talk, we have ignored our teacher's time for a bath. So, come. Let us be by his side.

(*Both exit. Enter the chamberlain.*)

Chamberlain:

> In the early part of his life,
> each householder strives for wealth,
> then the sons take on that task,
> and he can have some rest.
> As for me, this body withers
> with age and serving every day
> at chambers of the palace women—
> alas, a duty that is painful. (1)

(*Walks around.*)

I have been ordered by the king of Kashi's daughter, who has made a vow. 'For fulfilling it,' she said, 'I abjured pride and made a request to the great king through Nipunika. Convey my words to him again. Now, the evening worship is over,

and so I must see him.' (*Walks around and looks.*) Delightful
indeed is the scene of the royal palace at the end of the day:

> Peacocks, drowsy with sleep at night,
> sit like sculptures on the roof;
> wild pigeons there are confused by
> a net of incense smoke from widows;
> and the evening lamps, auspicious,
> are lit by ladies old and pious,
> who know this work and also make
> floral offerings at proper places. (2)

(*Looking backstage.*)

> Oh, here comes the king:
> surrounded by the torches held
> in the hands of maids, he shines
> like a winged mountain, moving
> with flowering trees upon its slopes. (3)

I will stay here so as to be seen.

(*Enter the king as described, with the jester.*)

King (*to himself*):

> Occupied with other work,

my day was spent without much trouble;
but how will this long night pass
in the absence of pleasant diversion? (4)

Chamberlain (*approaching the king*): Victory. O king. Victory! The queen entreats you. 'There is a beautiful moon to be seen from the roof of the Jewel Palace,' she says, 'I would like to be with the king when the Moon unites with Rohini, its constellation and consort.'

King: Please tell the queen, 'As you desire.'

Chamberlain: So will it be. (*Exits.*)

King: Comrade, is the queen really doing this to keep a vow?

Jester: Oh, I think that lady regrets having ignored your falling at her feet, and wishes to make up, with all these arrangements about a vow.

King: You are right, sir. For:

By ignoring my prostration,
her mind was set on fire,
and when it seeks reconciliation,
that proud woman feels ashamed. (5)

So, show the way to the terrace of the Jewel Palace.

Jester: This way, sir, this way. Go up by this marble staircase, glorious as the river Ganga. At its top is the terrace. It is delightful at this time of dusk.

King: Go ahead. (*Both mime climbing the stairs.*)

Jester: Oh, the moon is about to rise! A lovely light can be seen on the face of the eastern quarter, as it is now unveiled from darkness.

King: Well spoken, friend.

> The rays of a hidden moon, now rising,
> dispel darkness, like knotted tresses,
> from the face of the eastern quarter,
> and make my eyes its prisoner. (6)

Jester: Hey! Hey! The king of us twice-born folk has now risen. It is like a slice from a ball of sugar candy!ⁱⁱⁱ

King (*smiling*): For a glutton, eatables are everywhere! (*Folds hands and bows.*)

> O Lord of the Night,
> You stay by the sun for pious prayers,

all gods and ancestors, satisfy, [iv]
with libations of your nectar,
and dispel darkness of the night.
O crest-jewel of Shiva, I bow to you.   (7)

Jester: Sir, take a seat with the words prescribed by brahmins, as conveyed to you by your grandfather. Then, I too may sit at ease!

King (*accepts the jester's words and sits down, looking at the attendant maids*): When moonlight shines, where is the need for torches? Please rest yourselves.

Attendants: As the lord commands. (*They exit.*)

King (*gazing at the moon*): Friend, the queen's arrival may take some time. While we are alone, I would like to tell you something about my condition.

Jester: It is indeed quite visible. But, after seeing the love that Urvashi has shown you, it should be possible to sustain yourself with that bond of hope.

King: That is so. But the agony in my heart is also great:

See, the river's currant spreads
through hundreds of outlets,

till its flow is obstructed
by the presence of big rocks;
so too does the heart's love, when
the joy of union is denied. (8)

Jester: Your limbs look reduced, but even more splendid. I don't think your union with that beloved is too far away.

King (*marking an omen*): Comrade,

Your words do give rise to hope,
so does the throbbing in my right arm,[v]
that is very painful,
but also reassuring. (9)

Jester: Well, the word of a brahmin can never be otherwise.

(*Enter Urvashi, in the garb of a woman going on a tryst, and Chitralekha.*)

Urvashi (*looking at herself*): Will this dress for a tryst please you, friend Chitralekha? Just a few ornaments, with a blue silk bodice?

Chitralekha: I don't have enough words to praise it! But I know that I am not Pururavas.

Urvashi: Take me quickly to where that dear one lives. This is indeed the god of love's command for you!

Chitralekha: Well, we are already there, at the abode of your lover. It looks like the transformed peak of Mount Kailasa.[vi]

Urvashi: And where is that robber of my heart? What is he doing? Just find this out through your powers.

Chitralekha (*to herself*): Well, I will play a bit with her about this. (*Aloud.*) Friend, he is in a room for pleasure, enjoying it with the darling he desires.

(*Urvashi mimes dejection.*)

Chitralekha: You simpleton! What else can one say about his union with you, who are his darling?

Urvashi (*with a sigh*): My heart is sincere, but also suspicious.

Chitralekha: Well, here is that saintly king. At the Jewel Palace, with just one companion. Come, let us go near him.

(*Both descend.*)

King: Friend, the night deepens, and so does the pain of my love.

Urvashi: My heart trembles with his words, but they are not clear. Let us hide and hear them till our doubts are resolved.

Chitralekha: As you like.

Jester: Then, enjoy the nectar laden moonlight.

King: Comrade, this pain cannot be healed thus. Look,

> Not by a bed, with flowers strewn
> and with beams of moonlight,
> nor sandal paste on all the limbs,
> and a string of gems:
> only can that nymph divine
> relieve the torment of my heart,
> though it may be lightened by
> our private talk about her.   (10)

Urvashi: O my heart! You have got your reward by leaving me and joining him!

Jester: Yes! When I don't get my sweet yoghurt with mangoes, I too console myself by praying for them!

King: Friend, I feel the same.

Chitralekha: Listen! Not satisfied? Listen!

Jester: How could that be?

King:

> This shoulder, pressed against her,
> with the chariot's jolts:
> it alone is blessed in this body,
> the rest are a burden on this earth. (11)

Urvashi: Why delay this anymore? (*Rushes to the king.*) Friend Chitralekha, even though I now stand before him, that great king seems indifferent.

Chitralekha (*smiling*): You are so impatient! You forget that you are still invisible!

Voice Offstage: This way, Madam, this way.

(*All hear this. Urvashi and her friend are dejected.*)

Jester: Oh! Oh! The queen has arrived. Tongues should now be kept in check.

King: Your tongue too! Also hide your thoughts within yourself.

Urvashi: Friend, what do we do now?

Chitralekha: Not to worry. We are not visible to them. One can see that the royal spouse is dressed for keeping a vow. So she will not stay long.

(*Then enters the queen with attendants carrying oblations.*)

Queen: Oh! Oh! Nipunika. That deer-marked lord, the moon, looks more glorious in union with the constellation Rohini!

Maid: But it cannot surpass the glory of our lady with our great lord!

(*They walk around.*)

Jester (*seeing them*): Oh, the queen looks very good today. But I don't know if she is greeting me. Or, freed of resentment caused by the vow, she wants to make up with you.

King (*with a smile*): Both are possible. But your second sentence seems more likely to me. The lady,

> Wears a white silk garment,
> and is ornamented only
> with auspicious signs,
> like on her hair pure *durva*[vii] grass:
> her pride occasioned by that vow

now seems to have been given up,
and her person does appear
to be somewhat pleased with me. (12)

Queen (*approaching*): Victory to you, victory, noble one!

Attendants: Victory, victory, master!

Jester: Welcome. My lady.

King: Welcome, Queen!

(*Taking her hand, he seats her.*)

Urvashi: Friend, it is right to address her with the word 'queen'. She is no less than Shachi in splendour.[viii]

Chitralekha: Well said by you! And without jealousy!

Queen: I have to complete a special vow that concerns you, noble one. So, bear this botheration for an hour.

King: No, not so. It is indeed a favour, not a bother.

Jester: May there be more such favours, together with sweets.

King: What is the name of this queenly vow?

(*The queen looks at Nipunika.*)

Nipunika: Master, it is called 'Propitiation of the Beloved'.

King: If that is so,

> With this vow, O blessed one,
> for no reason you give pain
> to your lotus-stalk like tender body.
> Why do you so please this slave,
> who himself does seek your favour?　　　　　　(13)

Urvashi: His respect for her is indeed great.

Chitralekha: O you simpleton! Gentlemen, who love someone else, are even more courteous.

Queen: Is it the effect of this vow that you speak thus, noble one?

Jester: Stop, sir. It is not proper to contradict such nice words.

Queen: Maids, bring the offerings so that I may worship the moonbeams now on this Jewel Palace.

Attendants: As the queen commands, here are the offerings.

Queen (*miming worship of the moonbeams with flowers etc.*): Maids, give those blessed sweets to the noble Manavaka.

Attendants: As the queen commands. These are for you, noble Manavaka.

Jester (*taking the sweets*): May all be well, my lady. May your vow be very fruitful.

Queen: Come here, noble one.

King: Here I am.

Queen (*mimes worshipping the king and bows to him with folded hands*): That divine couple of Rohini and the Moon is my witness as I gratify you in turn, noble one. From today there will be a bond of affection between me and that woman whom you entreat and who wants to be yours.

Urvashi: Oh, I do not understand what her words mean. But my heart is now calmed and confident.

Chitralekha: Friend, that chaste and noble lady has consented to your union with that lover. Now it can take place!

Jester (*to himself*): When the fish escapes, and the fisherman loses a catch, 'Such is my duty,' he says, disappointed. And so is she. (*Aloud.*) O lady, is your lord so dear to you?

Queen: You fool! I want to soothe him. Even at the cost of my own happiness. Judge from this if he is dear or not dear to me.

King:

> You have the power
> to make me a slave,
> or give me away to another,
> but you are being very fearful,
> I am not at all
> as you suspect me to be. (14)

Queen: You may be or you may not. The vow of the lover's propitiation has now been completed. So, girls, let us go.

King: My dear, I will indeed not be propitiated, if you leave me and go away!

Queen: I never break rules, noble one.

(*Exits with her entourage.*)

Urvashi: Friend, that saintly king does love his wife. But I cannot take back my heart.

Chitralekha: What? Have you now lost hope?

King (*sitting down*): The queen could not have gone far, comrade.

Jester: Say frankly what you want to say. The doctor soon gives up a patient on judging him as incurable. So have you been, sir, by our lady.

King: Could Urvashi . . .

Urvashi: . . . be fulfilled today?

King:

> Could that dear one fill my ears
> with the secret tinkle of her anklets,
> and then slowly cover my eyes
> with the lotuses of her hands?
> Or, alighting on this palace,
> and moving slowly out of shyness,
> be brought firmly, step by step,
> by her clever friend to me? (15)

Urvashi: Friend, I will fulfil this, that is his desire.

(*Going behind him, covers the king's eyes. Chitralekha makes a sign to the jester.*)

King (*feeling her touch*): Friend, it is she. It is that beauty, born from the sage Narayana's thigh.

Jester: How could you know that?

King: How can I not know?

My body is by love tormented,
who else, by a touch of her hand
would be able to comfort it?
It is not with the sun's hot rays
that the lily blooms, but only
by moonbeams upon it. (16)

Urvashi (*removing her hands and coming a little before him*): Victory, great king, victory!

King: Welcome, O beauty. (*Sits with her on the same seat.*)

Chitralekha: Is my friend happy?

King: Indeed, so am I.

Urvashi: Friend, the queen gave the great king away. So, I have come to him like a lover. Don't think of me as an intruder.

Jester: What? Have you been here since sunset?

King (*looking at Urvashi*):

> If you come to this, my body,
> after the queen gave it away,
> then, with whose assent, did you
> at the beginning steal my heart? (17)

Chitralekha: Friend, she has no answer. But listen to my request.

King: I am all attention.

Chitralekha: Sir, as spring ends, I must now attend to the sun god in this hot season. But you must please do all to ensure that my fear friend does not start pining for heaven.

Jester: Why would she think of heaven? There one can neither eat nor drink, but only stare with unblinking eyes like a fish.

King: Gentle lady,

> Endless joys does heaven have,
> who can ever forget them?
> But Pururavas will be your slave,
> not that of another woman. (18)

Chitralekha: I am so grateful! Be strong, friend Urvashi. Give me leave.

Urvashi (*embracing Chitralekha*): Friend, do not forget me!

(*Chitralekha exits with a bow to the king.*)

Jester: Your wish has been fulfilled, sir. Congratulations.

King: She is indeed my fulfilment. Look,

> Friend, I have never been so content
> as I am today, obtaining
> service at her lovely feet:
> it's greater than my feet being adorned
> by the crest-jewels of other chiefs,
> or their parasols of sovereignty. (19)

Urvashi: I can't say anything sweeter than that!

King (*holding Urvashi's hand*): This fulfilment is incomparable.

> The same moonbeams now soothe my body,
> and the same darts of love do please,
> it is as if all that could troublesome be,
> is now, O beauty, my delight,
> in union with you. (20)

Urvashi: I was at fault to be late in coming to the great king.

King: No, not so.

> That which comes after the pain,
> is a greater happiness:
> as a tree's shade is more special
> to one oppressed by heat. (21)

Jester: Sir, we have enjoyed these lovely moonbeams. It is now time to go to the bedroom.

King: Then show the way to your friend.

Jester: This way, lady, this way.

(*They walk around.*)

King: O Beauty, now this is my request.

Urvashi: What is it?

King:

> With no fulfilment of desire,
> my night did lengthen hundredfold,
> but fair browed one, if in a union,

with you, it extends as long as that,
I will blessed be indeed. (22)

(*Exit all.*)

End of Act Three

Act Four

Singer Offstage:

Lonely at her separation
from a dear companion,
she is distraught and does weep
together with another friend,
as lotus flowers, touched by sunlight
are opening upon a lake.   (1)

(*Enter Sahajanya and Chitralekha.*)

Chitralekha (*enters step by step, looks at the sky*):

A pair of swans, both overcome
with sadness for their other halves,
and their eyes brimming with tears,
are lamenting on the lake.   (2)

Sahajanya: Friend Chitralekha, your face looks pale like a faded flower. It indicates a troubled heart. Tell me the cause, so that I may share the pain.

Chitralekha (*pitifully*): I was at prayers to the sun god as is traditional for us nymphs. It was the Spring Festival. But my dear friend was not there. I missed her greatly.

Sahajanya: I know you love one another. And, then?

Chitralekha: I went into a meditation and learnt that something terrible had happened that day.

Sahajanya: What was that, friend?

Chitralekha (*pitifully*): Urvashi took that saintly king, who had left affairs of state to his ministers, for some pleasure time at the forest of maddening scent, Gandhamadana, near the peak of Mount Kailasa.

Sahajanya (*with praise*): Friend, that is indeed a place for mutual enjoyment. And, then?

Chitralekha: There was a young woman playing about on the sandy banks of the river Mandakini.[i] She was Udayavati, the daughter of a demi-god. That royal sage stared at her for a long time. This enraged my dear friend Urvashi.

Sahajanya: Indeed, she could not have borne it. Her love had already risen to such a peak. So, this was bound to happen. And, then?

Chitralekha: She did not accept her lover's entreaties. Her mind had also been smitten by her guru's curse. Forgetting the rule laid down by the god Kumara,[ii] she entered his adjoining grove, that is forbidden to women. And there she got transformed into a creeper vine at the forest's edge.

Sahjanya (*sadly*): There is nothing beyond fate. It can lead even such love to such a result. And, then?

Chitralekha: The king is still in that forest, madly searching for his beloved. 'Here is Urvashi! There is she!' He cries, and spends both day and night there. But rain clouds are gathering in the sky. This can cause unease even to perfected souls, and I think will be worse for him.

Singer Offstage:

> A pair of swans
> on a limpid lake
> are so distressed
> for their missing partners
> that they are soaked

in endless tears
and overcome by pain. (3)

Sahajanya: Such noble souls can never suffer long. Some blessing will definitely lead them to a reunion. So, come, let us pray to the divine sun that is about to rise.

Singer Offstage:

Its mind filled with worry,
and longing for the partner,
a swan wanders on the lake,
lonely midst the blooming lotuses. (4)

(*Exit of nymphs as the song ends.*)

Entrance Song Offstage:

That lord of regal elephants,
looking sick and maddened
at separation from his darling,
now enters a forest grove,
his body adorned with
blooming sprouts from trees. (5)

(*The king enters with the song, looking madly at the sky.*)

King: Stop, wicked demon, stop! Where are you taking my beloved? (*Looking up.*) What is this? He has flown from the mountain peak into the sky, and showers me with arrows. (*Picks up a lump of earth, and runs to strike, but stops and looks around.*)

Singer Offstage:

> A young swan is
> lamenting on the lake,
> with tearful eyes
> and flapping wings,
> his heart grief-stricken
> for his beloved. (6)

King (*looks closely, then says pitifully*):

> This is a new cloud that I see,
> not a dark and armoured demon;
> this indeed is a rainbow,
> not the bow by an archer drawn;
> this too is a shower of rain,
> not a volley of arrows;
> and that golden streak is lightning,
> not my darling Urvashi. (7)

(*Faints and falls, then gets up sighing.*)

> I thought that my doe-eyed girl
> was abducted by a demon;
> that was but a great dark cloud
> raining down with lightning flashes.   (8)

(*Pitifully wondering where she could have gone.*)

> She was enraged, and does now stand,
> invisible, with her special powers,
> but she cannot for long stay angry,
> for her heart holds love for me.
> Did she fly away to heaven?

(*With anger.*)

> Even the foes of gods cannot
> take her away from me,
> but to my eyes she still is lost,
> can this be my destiny?   (9)

(*Looks, with tears and sighs, in all directions.*)

> Alas, pain does follow pain
> for those struck by misfortune,
> the day may cool, delightful turn

with advent of rain-clouds new,
but, on the other hand, separation
from my dearest is still unbearable.   (10)

(*Sings and dances the Charchari.*)[iii]

Stop! O Cloud! What have you started?
It's a rain unending that covers the sky.
Still, while roaming on this earth,
if I can see her, my beloved,
whatever then that you may do,
I will put up with all of it.   (11)

(*Thinking about this song.*)

To ignore this growing pain in my heart is indeed useless.
But, if even sages say that the king decides the time fit for
each action, can't I forbid the cloud to rain? (*Laughs, repeating
the sages' words.*) Even sages say that the king decides the time
fit for each action. So be it. I forbid the cloud!

In spring, the wish-fulfilling trees
dance with many lovely ripples
of their bud-clusters in the breeze,
whose fragrance does madden the bees
that buzz, with echoes from the cuckoos.   (12)

(*Dances to this song.*)

But I should not forbid it, when these signs of rain are good for my kingdom. (*Laughs and again dances to that song.*) And, how is that?

> That cloud with golden lightning flashes,
> is my royal canopy, and beneath it
> the *nichula*[iv] trees are also waving
> their floral fans for me;
> the peacocks, with their voices raised
> at summer's end are my bards,
> and hills are courtiers offering gifts
> from their rain-splashed ridges.
> But what is the use of any such talk?
> First, I must for my loved one search. (13)

Another Singer Offstage:

> Without his mate, the pain is greater,
> now movements hampered, by separation:
> and the wanderings of that lord of elephants
> have slackened in a hill bright with flowers. (14)

(*The king walks and looks around slowly, then speaks with joy.*)

King: Oh! Oh! This strengthens my resolve! And, how is that?

These new flowers on plantain trees,
red-lined and moist with the rain,
do remind me of her eyes,
wet with angry tears.   (15)

But how can I know if she did actually pass this way?

If that beauty's feet did touch the earth,
the sandy soil where it had rained
in this forest would show the prints
of those feet beneath her comely hips.   (16)

(*Walks and looks around slowly, then joyfully speaks.*)

Oh! Oh! Here are some signs of the path that enraged woman
followed.

Here, dark-green as a parrot's belly,
is the bodice from her breasts,
stained with colour from her lips,
and the tear drops from her eyes
that rushed down as she walked in anger.   (17)

So be it. I will pick it up. (*Walks about, then tearfully.*)
What? What is this? Only some fresh green grass with red
rain beetles? Then, where in this forest has my darling gone?
(*Looking.*) Oh, there is a peacock upon a rock on that hillside.

It looks at the clouds, as gusts of wind
do make its crest feathers dance,
and raises its neck to then emit
the hooting cry of peacocks. (18)

(*Approaching it.*) Let me ask it.

Singer Offstage:

In a state of deep depression,
and in a hurry to relieve it,
longing for the vision of
his loved one, the elephant
is filled with much confusion. (19)

King (*dances and sings*):

O peacock, I beg of you,
tell me please, if you did see
my loved one roaming in this forest.
She is like the moon at night
and has a swan-like gait:
you will know her by these signs
told to you by me. (20)

(*Sits down with folded hands after the dance.*)

O blue-necked bird, my anxious longing
for that long-eyed and fair-limbed maid,
who, if in this forest was seen by you,
would be a favour to my sight.   (21)

(*Dances, then looks.*)

What? He does not reply, but begins to dance!

(*Dances and sings again.*)

What is the cause of his joy? Ah, I know:

He is now without a rival,
with the bright cloud of his plumage
rippling in a gentle breeze.
But if that girl of beautiful locks,
let loose in the play of love
into her hands, was now here,
what would this peacock do?   (22)

Well, I will not ask one who has no time for problems of
others. (*Walks and looks around.*) Ah! Here is a cuckoo,
stimulated by the end of the hot season, on a black plum
jambu tree. She is the cleverest of birds, and I will ask her.

Singer Offstage:

Surrounded by a grove divine,
heaving painful sighs of sorrow
with all joy banished from the heart,
the elephant lord moves like a cloud. (23)

King (*singing and dancing the Charchari*):

O sweet singing cuckoo, dear,
tell me if she was seen by you,
my sweetheart roaming by herself
in the garden of paradise. (24)

(*After dancing and whirling, the king falls to his knees.*)

King: Madam,

Lovers do call you Kama's emissary,
his weapon immaculate, and an expert
at breaking down the other's pride:
so, bring my darling close to me,
or lead me, you sweet-voice, to where she is. (25)

(*He whirls a bit and looks to the sky.*)

What did you say? 'How could she go, leaving a lover like you?' Listen, Madam:

> She is angry: but I do not recall
> even once giving her cause
> for any anger—but this is the way
> for women to exert mastery
> on lovers by a show of feelings.   (26)

(*Sits down, confused, then rises to his knees and repeats the previous verse, looking above.*)

What is this? She has broken off our talk to look at her own self. Is such behaviour proper?

> Even the pain, though great, of another,
> is a trifle, as the proverb says,
> and ignoring my request
> that bird is in herself absorbed,
> she sucks a fruit of the black plum tree
> as if it is the lip of her mate.   (27)

Even so, I am not angry with her, whose sweet voice is like that of my beloved. Be happy, my lady. Now, let us move on. (*Gets up carefully.*) Oh! To the right of this row of trees is a tinkle of anklets like the one that comes from the steps of my beloved. I will follow it. (*Walks around.*)

Singer Offstage:

> The face paled at the loved one's parting,
> the eyes brimming with endless tears,
> the gait stricken with pain unbearable,
> and all the body in it burning,
> the elephant lord in that forest wanders,
> with its heart even more depressed. (28)

(*The king dances in all six directions, then carefully looks all around. The offstage song continues.*)

> Of his loved one bereft,
> burning in terrible grief,
> the eyes overflowing with tears,
> that elephant wanders in a daze. (29)

King (*pitifully*): A curse on this pain!

> But, that was the tweet of a royal swan,
> keen to get to the Manasa lake,
> on seeing dark clouds in the sky:
> not the tinkle of my darling's anklet. (30)

So be it. As these birds are keen to get to the lake, they do fly away. But get me some news of my beloved. (*Dances and falls to his knees.*)

O mountain birds,
Before you fly away to that lake,
do drop those lotus stalks you carry,
and pick up others again,
But rescue me from this distress
with some news of my beloved:
good folks listen to others too
before minding their own interests.   (31)

(*Sits down, ready to dance.*)

Oh, the way that bird is looking ahead clearly means: 'She
was not seen by me, for my mind is busy with travel.'

(*Gets up, dancing.*)

If, O swan, you did not see
my darling with her curving brows
pass by on that lake's shore,
O thief how did you then acquire
her playful but stately gait?   (32)

(*Dances again and comes forward with folded hands.*)

Swan, give back my loved one,
whose movements you have stolen:

by law, if a part is taken,
the whole must be returned. (33)

(*Dances again.*)

Longing to learn how that girl walked
when did you view her rolling hips? (34)

(*Again a dance as the king repeats and acts the verse with a laugh.*)

The bird has fled out of fear that the king will punish it. I must now look for some other alternative. (*Walks and looks around.*) Oh, here is a *chakravaka*, a ruddy goose with his mate. I will ask him. (*Dances in different styles.*)

Singer Offstage (*the king dances the Kutilika*)ᵛ:

His mind stolen by their ripples,
(*He dances the Mallaghati.*)
as flowers bloom on best of trees,
(*Dances the Charchari.*)
maddened by his love's separation,
the elephant lord in the forest roams. (35)

King (*dancing another Charchari*):

O ruddy goose of golden colour,
Please do speak to me.
Did you my loved one behold,
as by the lake she played about?   (36)

(*Dances and falls to his knees.*)

This chariot rider questions you,
one who has the name of a chariot wheel,[vi]
and he is filled with many emotions
since abandoned by one who has
hips as round as a chariot wheel.   (37)

'Who, who is that?' he says.
Indeed, he does not know who I am.
I whose mother's father is the Sun god,
and father's father, god of the Moon,
one who is the lover-master
of Urvashi, and lord of the Earth.   (38)

But, what is this? It stays silent. I need to overwhelm it.
(*Falling to his knees.*) It is proper that you should know what
happened to me. And how,

You get anxious, and do weep,
worried that your mate is far away,

though she is just hidden by
a leaf of the lotus on the lake.
This is your love, and also fear
of separation from your partner:
then why is it that you ignore
my feelings of lovelorn distress?   (39)

(*Sitting down.*) Such is always the effect of misfortune upon me. (*Getting up.*) Oh!

It torments me, that buzzing sound
of the bee within a lotus bloom,
it's like the murmur of her mouth
when her lip is bitten by me.   (40)

To avoid any regret when it leaves, I will now ask that bee which is enjoying the lotus.

Singer Offstage (*as the king assumes half of a dancing pose*):

As enhanced by one another,
increased is their flow of love:
that young swan upon the lake
is sporting under Kama's sway.   (41)

King (*sitting down in a full dance pose with folded hands*):

O bee, you would praise the ways
of my darling with her eyes like wine,
but have not yet beheld her person.
If you had the fragrance smelt
of the breath pervading from her lips,
would you still love this white lotus?   (42)

(*Walks around and looks carefully.*)

Well, there stands the king of elephants, with his mate beside him and his trunk resting on a branch of a kadamba[vii] tree. From him may I get news of my beloved, and so should approach him gently.

Singer Offstage (*as the king dances Kutilika*):

He burns in grief
at the loss of his love,
(*He dances the Mallaghati.*)
in the forest, brushing
a bee off his temple.   (43)

(*The king looks around after dancing.*)

King: But this may not be the best time to approach him.

He seeks the wine that is the juice
of a just plucked budding fruit,
to him offered with her trunk
by his loved one from a broken branch.   (44)

(*Assumes a dance pose and looks.*)

He has now finished eating it. So I will go near him and ask.

(*Another Charchari dance.*)

O great elephant, who can break
big trees with a playful blow,
please tell me, as I ask of you,
did you see my love passing by,
she, whose glow outshines the moon.   (45)

(*Takes two steps to come before the elephant.*)

O rutting lord of the elephant herd,
did you have the pleasure of a glimpse
of that woman in her prime of youth,
her hair with jasmine flowers strung,
gleaming like a crescent moon
that may be seen from far?   (46)

(*Listens joyfully.*)

Ah! His rumbling cry reassures me with news of my beloved.
You are like me. And I love her:

> I am called the king of kings,
> and you the lord of elephants,
> your flow of rut does please the bees,
> and my charity the supplicants,
> Urvashi, that gem of a woman,
> is my love, as that mate is yours,
> but my pain is due to her separation:
> may you never feel the same. (47)

Sir, may you have all joy.

(*Walks and carefully looks around.*)

Oh, here is that special hill called the Scented Caves.
Delightful, it is loved by nymphs. Perhaps my beloved can be
found nearby.

(*Walks around and looks.*)

How dark it has become! So be it. I will look by the lightning
flashes. What? As a result of my misdoings, even clouds have
lost their lightning! But I must not turn back without asking
that mountain peak.

Singer Offstage:

> Look at that wild boar
> standing in a dense forest,
> engaged in its own work
> of digging earth with sharp claws. (48)

King:

> O mountain with colossal sides,
> that lady of delicate limbs
> may be resting in your forest dense:
> is she, who has such delicate hips,
> now inside that grove of Kama? (49)

What is this? It stays silent? I wonder if it does not hear me because of the distance. Very well, I will go closer and ask.

(*Dances the Charchari.*)

> O mountain, who upholds the earth,
> has waterfalls flowing through marble rocks,
> all kinds of flowers on its peak,
> and demi-gods singing, sweet enchantments,
> do show me my dearest love. (50)

(*The king dances the Charchari with folded hands.*)

O lord of all hills on the earth,
was that beauty seen by you?
One lovely in all her limbs,
dwelling in this forest grove,
when on being from me separated? (51)

(*Hears an echo of his words, and listens with joy.*)

What? He says she was seen as I described! Very well, I will search for her. (*Looks at the sky, and speaks sadly.*) What? That was only an echo of my own words?

(*Faints and falls, then gets up and sits sadly.*)

Oh, I am tired. Will sit by this mountain river's bank, to feel the breeze from its waves. (*Walks and looks carefully.*) A look at this flow full of turbid water arouses my desire. Why?

That wave is like her frowning brow,
the flustered birds her girdle bells,
the foam her skirt now being pulled
after being loosened in excitement:
thus does she go, feeling greatly cheated,
like the river flow that cannot bear the rock. (52)

Very well. I will please the river.

(*He dances the Kutulika.*)

> O river, so dear and beautiful,
> be pleased with bows from frightened birds,
> and that eager black buck upon
> your bank divine, and buzzing bees. (53)

(*Dances the Charchari.*)

> Stricken by an eastern wind,
> the waves, his arms, have risen up,
> in the sea-lord's charming dance with clouds,
> with saffron conch-shells ornamented,
> and stirred by sharks and crocodiles,
> dark hued like the lotus black:
> the hands of the tide provide a beat.
> and new rain showers cover the sky. (54)

(*After dancing, the king falls to his knees.*)

> In love for you, are my words sweet,
> my heart opposes a break in love,
> what sign of fault did you see in me,
> O proud one, to renounce this slave? (55)

What is this? She is silent! Or, perhaps it is just a river, and not my Urvashi at all. Otherwise how could she abandon

Pururavas to join the ocean? But, can the best be obtained without despair? So, I will go the very place where those beautiful eyes disappeared from mine. (*Walks around to look.*) And I will ask that spotted deer sitting by the river about news of my beloved.

> Besides that big tree with new flowers,
> charming with coos of mating cuckoos,
> Airavata, king of elephants, roams,
> burning in fires of separation
> from its mate, in the garden of paradise. (56)

(*The king drops to his knees.*)

> That mirage of a spotted deer
> does look like a sidelong glance
> flashed by the goddess of this grove
> to show the splendour of the forest. (57)

(*Observing.*)

> But the deer only looks at its doe, approaching
> from behind with a nursing fawn,
> and as such a little hindered.
> It has no sight for anything else. (58)

(*Dances the Charchari.*)

My love is in the prime of youth,
with slim body, shapely hips,
swelling and still rising breasts,
and a loveliness divine;
if that doe-eyed girl was by you seen
roaming in this bright skied forest,
then please do rescue me
from this ocean of separation.   (59)

(*With hands folded in supplication.*)

O lord of the deer folk,
was my beloved seen by you
in this forest? I will tell you
her distinctive features, listen:
she has large eyes, just like your mate,
and looks just as beautiful.   (60)

(*Observing the deer.*)

What is this? He just keeps looking at its mate, with no consideration for my words? I must look for some other possibility.

(*Walks around looking.*)

Here is a red kadamba tree,
that marks the end of summer's heat,

she used its still uneven blooms
to ornament her hair. (61)

(*Walks around and looks.*) But what is that in the cleft of a rock? It looks extremely red!

But it glows, so is not some flesh
of an elephant by a lion killed,
nor is it a spark of fire,
as there has been a heavy rain:
O it is a precious stone
ruby red like a blooming flower,
and put there as if by solar rays. (62)

Well, I will take it.

Singer Offstage (*as the king mimes picking up that red object*):

His hopes, bound to his beloved,
his eyes brimming with tears
and face worn out with grief,
in the forest roams that elephant lord. (63)

(*The king takes the gem carefully, then to himself.*)

King: It should be put upon her hair plait

that is scented with coral flowers,
but when my love is hard to find,
I will not spoil it with my tears. (64)

Voice Offstage: Take it, son, take it.

This uniting gem has come
from paint on the mountain lady's feet:
it brings for one who puts it on
a speedy union with the loved one. (65)

King (*listening*): Who indeed gives me this command? (*Looking in that direction*) O it is some godly sage, moving like a deer, that has pitied me. I am grateful for your advice, sir. (*Takes the gem.*) O Gem of Reunion,

She of a slender waist has left me,
and if our reunion through you happens,
then I will make you my crest-jewel, sir,
like the crescent is of the great god. (66)

(*Walks and looks around.*) Why is it that, on seeing that creeper vine, my desire is aroused? It has no flowers, but my mind rejoices. For,

Its leaves are moist in the rain,
like my slim one's lips with tears,

at this time, it has no flowers,
like she, had no jewels, in our separation;
with no bees, its silent worries
are made known without any words:
as if, having left me at her feet,
that wrathful one burns now with remorse.   (67)

So, I will be its lover, and embrace this creeper, that imitates
my beloved.

O creeper vine, on seeing you,
I do feel with all my heart
that if fated to get her back,
I will free her from all doubts,
so that she never leaves me.   (68)

(*Dancing the Charchari, he approaches the creeper and embraces
it. Then, enter Urvashi.*)

King (*with eyes closed, mimics touching her*): Oh! On this
touch of Urvashi, my body is filled with bliss! But I have
no faith.

When I accept it as my love,
it quickly something else becomes,
so I will not suddenly open eyes,
and still think it my darling's touch.   (69)

(*Slowly opens his eyes.*)

What? It is really Urvashi?

(*Faints and falls down.*)

Urvashi: Take heart, great king, take heart!

King (*regaining consciousness*): Darling, I am alive!

> O Chandi,[viii] in your separation,
> I was drowning in the dark,
> now, by fate, you have come back
> like spirit within one who was gone.　　　　(70)

Urvashi: Forgive, forgive me, great king! It was my getting angry that got you into this terrible condition.

King: I do not deserve to be propitiated by you. Your sight has delighted both my body and soul. But tell me, how could you stay separated from me for so long?

(*Dances the Charchari.*)

> Peacock, cuckoo, swan, red goose,
> bee, elephant, mountain, river, deer—

whom did I not ask for you,
as I wandered weeping in this forest? (71)

Urvashi: So it was, great king. What you did could be seen in my inner mind.

King: Inner mind? Darling I don't understand.

Urvashi: Listen, great king. Long ago the great soldier god Kumara had taken a vow of eternal chastity. Living near the untainted grove at Gandhamadana, he had set a boundary around it.

King: What kind of boundary?

Urvashi: It was that if any woman were to enter this area, she would be transformed into a creeper vine. And she would not be released from that state without the gem formed from the paint on the goddess Gauri's feet. I went inside the god Kumara's grove. My mind had been maddened by the guru's curse, and I had forgotten the rule that god had ordained. And, after entering it, I was transformed into a creeper vine at the edge of the grove.

King: My love, all this makes some sense.

But, when, exhausted by our love-making,
I slept, you would think I had gone away:
how could you have born this long separation,
unless it had been thus decreed? (72)

And here is the so-called means of our reunion. We too now
know its power.

(*Shows her the gem.*)

Urvashi: What? Is this the Gem of Reunion? That is why,
after your embrace, I am back in my actual form.

King (*touches the gem to his forehead*):

By the colour and glow emitted
from this gem on your forehead placed,
your face does now display the splendour
of a red lotus in the light of dawn. (73)

Urvashi: So lovingly said. But it is a long time since we came
out of the city of Pratishthana. Sometime people complain
about our absence. So, come, let us go.

King: As you say, my lady.

(*Both get up.*)

Urvashi: How would the great king wish to go?

King:

> O you of a milk-like face,
> take me to our new home
> by that stately flying chariot,
> splendid with new rainbows,
> and lightning flashes as the flag.　　　　　　(74)

Song Offstage (*in the style of a Charchari*):

> With his companion regained,
> and limbs bristling with joy,
> in an aerial chariot as requested,
> the young swan is now merry.　　　　　　(75)

(*Both exit to this song.*)

End of Act Four

Act Five

(*Enter the royal jester, overjoyed.*)

Jester: Hey! Hey! Thank God! My dear friend has come back! After enjoying himself with Urvashi for a long time in the divine groves, especially Nandana Vana, the garden of paradise. And once more he rules the kingdom, gratifying the subjects with his own supervision of regal affairs. Now, he has nothing to regret except the absence of an heir. Today is a special day. Having had the ritual bath, along with his queens, at the confluence of the sacred rivers Ganga and Yamuna, he has now entered the royal tent. So, while he is being anointed and ornamented, I too will go there to be one of the first among his attendants. (*Walks around.*)

Maid (*voice offstage*):

Alas! Alas! That gem was to be the crest-jewel for that luxury loving nymph. I had put it in a palm leaf basket, covered with a silk scarf. But a vulture thought it was a piece of meat and snatched it with a swoop.

Jester (*listening to the voice*): Terrible! That was the much prized crest-jewel of my friend, also known as the Gem of Reunion. And that royal lord has now got up from his seat before his toilet could be completed. So, I will go to his side.

(*Enter the king with his charioteer, chamberlain, huntress and other attendants.*)

King: Hunters! Hunters!

Where is that bird, also a robber,
that is seeking its own death,
by this theft, the very first,
in the house of its own protector? (1)

Huntress: There it is. Circling in the sky and brightening it with that gem, attached to a golden chain held in its beak.

King: I see it!

That chain of gold hangs from its beak,
and the bird makes circles in the sky
swinging the gem in an orbit swift,
bright with rays like a firework. (2)

106

What can be done?

Jester (*coming close*): No mercy here. The culprit must be punished.

King: Well said. Bring me the bow.

Attendant: As you command, sir.

King: But the bird can't be seen now.

Jester: That wretched vulture has now flown southwards.

King: Now I see it.

> With the rays of light that the gem emits
> that bird does now decorate the sky,
> as is done to a loved one's face
> with golden blooms of ashoka trees. (3)

(*Enter Yavani, a Greek woman bow-bearer.*)

Yavani: Master, here is your bow and the glove for it.

King: What is the bow's use, now? That carnivorous bird has gone beyond the range of an arrow. See,

That precious gem, now carried off
by that bird so far away,
now does gleam like the planet Mars
among dense clouds at night. (4)

(*Looks at the chamberlain.*) Noble Latavya, on my orders tell citizens to hunt down that robber bird when it goes to the tree where it roosts in the evening.

Chamberlain: As you command, sir. (*Exits.*)

Jester: Sir, now you should sit down. Where can that jewel-thief go to escape your orders?

King (*sitting down with the jester*):

Friend, my liking for the gem,
which was stolen by that bird,
is not just that it is a jewel,
but because it is that Gem of Reunion
which united me with my love. (5)

(*Enter the chamberlain with the gem and an arrow.*)

Chamberlain: Victory! Victory, my lord.

That condemned bird, it's body pierced
by your wrath, as well as an arrow,
in punishment just, did fall from the sky
together with that crest-jewel.   (6)

(All look surprised.)

Chamberlain: Once it has been washed, to whom should I give this gem?

King: Huntress, purify it in fire and then put it into a casket.

Huntress: As the master commands.

(Takes the gem and exits.)

King: Latavya, do you know whose arrow this is?

Chamberlain: It shows a name marked on it. But, with my sight I can't make it out.

King: Then bring that arrow to me.

(Chamberlain does so, and the king reads the name lovingly, as would be done by a parent.)

Chamberlain: Meanwhile, I will finish my work.

Jester: What are you thinking, sir?

King: Listen to the name of that arrow's shooter:

> This arrow belongs to that bow's wielder,
> prince Ayush, born of Urvashi,
> an offspring of the house of Ila,[i]
> and destroyer of enemies. (7)

Jester (*joyfully*): Fortune has favoured you with a son!

King: Friend, how could this be? Apart from the sacrificial ceremony in the Naimisha forest, I was never away from Urvashi. Nor did I ever see any sign of pregnancy on her. How could this birth have taken place? But,

> Her body did, for some days only,
> show darkened nipples on the breasts,
> a face as pale as a leaf of *lavali*,[ii]
> and there was some dullness in her eyes. (8)

Jester: Sir, you shouldn't imagine all human qualities to be present in celestial women. Their ways are hidden by their powers.

King: It may be as you say, sir. But what could be the reason for that lady hiding the son?

Jester: Maybe she thought: 'The king will abandon me, now an old woman.'

King: Enough of such jokes. Think!

Jester: Who can guess heavenly secrets?

(*Enter the chamberlain.*)

Chamberlain: Victory! Noble lord! Victory! My lord, a hermit woman has come here from the hermitage of the sage Chyavana, along with a boy. She wants to see you.

King: Let both of them come in without delay.

Chamberlain: As the noble lord commands.

(*Exits, and returns with the hermit woman and a boy carrying a bow.*)

Chamberlain: This way, lady. This way.

(*All go round the stage.*)

Jester (*looking*): Could this be the warrior boy whose name is marked on that crescent headed arrow? He looks very much like you.

King: It may be so. And, indeed:

> My gaze now is filled with tears,
> and my heart with love paternal,
> while the mind is overjoyed.
> My steadfast nature is disturbed
> and my limbs begin to tremble
> as I want him in a close embrace. (9)

Chamberlain: Reverend lady, stand here.

(*The hermit woman and the boy wait.*)

King: Reverend lady, I salute you.

Hermit Woman: Illustrious sir, may you extend the lunar line. (*To herself.*) Oh, even though he wasn't told, this saintly king knows his fatherly connection with this boy. (*Speaking aloud.*) Child, bow to your father.

(*The boy does so, with the bow between his folded hands.*)

King: May you live long.

Boy (*to himself*):

> If such love appears, and just on hearing
> that he is my father, I his son,
> what kind would it have been if grown
> in the father's fondling over years?　　　(10)

King: Reverend lady, what is the reason for your visit?

Hermit Woman: Listen, great king. This blessed boy Ayush was born to Urvashi. After that, for some reason she entrusted him to my care. The natal and other sacred rites for this warrior prince were arranged by the revered hermit Chyavana. Then, after the usual studies, he was instructed in the science of archery.

King: He has indeed been looked after well.

Hermit Woman: But today, when he went out with other hermit boys for flowers and fuel, his behaviour was contrary to that of the hermitage.

Jester: What was that?

Hermit Woman: A vulture, sitting with a piece of meat on top of a tree, was targeted and struck down by him with an arrow.

(*Jester looks at the king.*)

King: What then?

Hermit Woman: On getting news of this occurrence, the sage Chyavana instructed me to send back this ward of mine. So, I want to meet Urvashi.

King: Latavya, let Urvashi be called.

Chamberlain: As the lord commands. (*Exits.*)

King (*looking at the boy*): Come, boy, come here.

> They say that with the touch of a son
> the whole body does get a thrill,
> as happens to the moonstone gem
> when touched by the rays of the moon. (11)

Hermit Woman: Son, gladden your father.

(*The boy goes to the king and touches his feet.*)

King (*embracing the boy, and seating him on the footstool*): Child, this brahmin is your father's dear friend. Don't be afraid, salute him.

Jester: What will he fear? He lives in a hermitage and recognizes a monkey!

Boy (*saluting*): Dear sir, I salute you.

Jester: Be well, son!

(*Then enter Urvashi with the chamberlain.*)

Chamberlain: This way, my lady, this way.

Urvashi (*looking at the boy*): Who is this boy, sitting with a bow on the royal footstool? The top knot of his hair is being tied by the king himself. (*Then on seeing the hermit woman.*) Oh! The presence of Satyavati makes clear that it is our own little son, Ayush. He has grown so big! (*Walks around.*)

King (*looking at Urvashi*):

> Here comes one who gave you birth,
> in gazing at you she is now absorbed,
> with the bodice on her breast
> damp with the flowing milk of love.   (12)

(*The boy goes towards Urvashi.*)

Urvashi: Lady mother, I salute you.

Hermit Woman: Daughter, may you be honoured by your husband.

Boy: Mother, I greet you.

Urvashi (*embracing the boy and lifting up his face*): Son, adore your father. (*Approaching the king.*) Victory! Victory to the great king.

King: Welcome to the mother. Be seated here. (*Gives her half of his own seat. Urvashi sits there, and all others sit appropriately.*)

Hermit Woman: This Ayush has finished his studies, and is now fit to wear armour. So, I am handing him back to you in the presence of your lord. And I now wish to be relieved of this work, that interferes with my other duties at the hermitage.

Urvashi: Having seen you after a long time, I am already anxious that I will lose you. But it will not be proper to detain you from your duties. Noble lady, do go. Till I see you again!

King: Mother, please convey my respects to the sage Chyavana.

Hermit Woman: So be it.

Boy: Noble lady, if you are truly going back, then take me to the hermitage too.

King: Child, you have already spent the first stage of life there. The time has now come for you to enter the second.

Hermit Woman: Son, follow the words of your father.

Boy: Then,

> Send to me, my peacock, blue-necked,
> with its tail plumage now full grown,
> it slept in my lap, obtaining pleasure
> at my caressing it on the crest. (13)

Hermit Woman (*with a laugh*): I will do that! May you all be happy. (*Exits.*)

King (*to Urvashi*): Blessed beauty,

> I am today the happiest of fathers,
> with this fine son born of you:
> like Indra, conqueror of cities,
> is with Jayanta, son of Paulomi.[iii] (14)

(*Urvashi remembers something and weeps.*)

Jester: The lady has suddenly become tearful! Why?

King (*with concern*):

> Why, O Beauty, do you weep,
> shedding tears, like a string of pearls,
> upon your high and swelling breasts,
> when I have been with great joy filled
> at the birth that does continue my line? (15)

(*Wipes her tears.*)

Urvashi: Listen, great king. With this joy at seeing our son, I had forgotten something. But, with your praise of Indra, my order from him is now back in my mind.

King: What was that order?

Urvashi: In the past, great king, when you captured my heart, I was also commanded by the great Indra.

King: What was that command?

Urvashi: It was, 'When my dear friend sees the face of his progeny born through you, you must come back to me.' Then, afraid of losing you, as soon as that boy was born, I secretly placed him in the hands of that noble Satyavati for his studies at the sage Chyavana's hermitage. Today, as that boy, may he live long, was returned to me, she also said that he is now capable of serving his father. And that is the end of my stay with the great king.

(*All mime despair.*)

King (*with a sigh*): Oh, the contradiction between happiness and fate!

> I am consoled by having a son,
> but you, lean one, will go away:
> just as the first rain from a cloud
> soothes a tree suffering in heat,
> but the fire from its lightning flash
> can then burn it down. (16)

Jester: So, this has led to one calamity after another. Now I suppose that our lord must put on a garment of tree bark, and go to an ascetic grove.

Urvashi: I too am unfortunate. Having got back his son, whose studies are over, the great king has to go through all this, and I have to go up to heaven.

King: No, O beauty, not this,

Stay on, by orders of this husband—
it is not easy to do what one wants
in conditions of such separation:
I too will hand the kingdom over,
to our son, this Ayush, and
live in forests where deer herds roam.   (17)

Boy: Dear Father, it is not worthwhile to yoke a calf to a cart meant for a bull!

King: Dear Son,

An elephant in rut, though just a calf,
can other elephants subdue,
the venom of a baby snake,
still takes effect most speedily,
even a king, though but a boy,
can well protect the earth:
the competence to do one's duty
comes not from age but lineage.   (18)

Latavya, on my behalf, tell the assembly of ministers to make preparations for Ayush's coronation as king.

Chamberlain: As the godly king commands.

(*Exits sadly, as all mime being dazzled by a light.*)

King (*looking at the sky*): What is this flash of lightning from a cloudless sky?

Urvashi (*also looking*): Oh, it is the blessed lord Narada!ⁱᵛ

King: O blessed lord Narada! One who is,

> With matted and tawny hair,
> of the colour like some sulphur,
> and a sacred thread like the crescent moon:
> he is like a wish-fulfilling tree that moves
> with golden branches decked with pearls.   (19)

Bring for him an offering!

Urvashi (*bringing the needful*): Here is the offering for the blessed one.

(*Then enter Narada.*)

Narada: O ruler of the middle world, may you be victorious.

King (*taking the material from Urvashi's hands, and offering it*): Greetings, blessed lord.

Urvashi: I too salute the blessed one.

Narada: May you both be a couple inseparable!

King (*to himself*): Could that be so? (*Aloud, embracing the boy.*) Child, greet the blessed lord.

Boy: Blessed one! Ayush, the son of Urvashi, salutes you.

Narada: May you live long.

King: Please favour this seat.

Narada: Of course.

(*All sit around Narada.*)

King (*prayerfully*): Blessed lord, what is the purpose of your visit?

Narada: O king, listen to this message of the great Indra.

King: I am all attention.

Narada: To you sir, who have made up your mind to go to the forest, the mighty Indra has given this advice.

King: What does he command?

Narada: In his words: 'The sages who see all the three times, the past, the present and the future, have foretold an impending conflict between the gods and the demons. You, sir, are our helper in battle. As such, weapons of war should not be given up by you. And, as long as you live, this Urvashi will be your lawful spouse.'

Urvashi (*to herself*): Oh! It is as if a dart has been pulled out from my heart!

King: I remain at the disposal of the lord of the gods.

Narada: Good!

> Your work will be done by great Indra,
> and you should do what he prefers:
> as the sun does the fire kindle
> and the fire to it gives the glow. (20)

(*Looks at the sky.*)

O Rambha, bring here the things that the great Indra has himself put together for the anointment of Prince Ayush as the heir-apparent.

(*Rambha enters.*)

Rambha: Here are the things for that anointment.

Narada: Seat this boy with a long life on that auspicious seat.

Rambha: Here, child. (*Seats the boy.*)

Narada (*pouring a pitcher over the boy's head*): Rambha, complete the rest of this ceremony.

Rambha (*doing as told*): Child, salute the divine sage and your parents.

(*The boy salutes them in due order.*)

Narada: May you be blessed.

King: May you bear the yoke of the family.

Urvashi: May you please your father.

(*Two bards offstage.*)

First Bard: Victory, crown-prince:

> As the sage immortal Atri, son
> of Brahma, and the Moon of Atri,
> as Budha of the cool-rayed Moon,

and Budha's son,[v] this godly king:
so may you be, just like your father,
by your merits light the world,
and fulfil all blessings to your line.   (21)

Second Bard:

Your father, highest of the high,
and you of unshakable courage,
now share this glorious sovereignty,
which is splendid even more
than the waters of the Ganga
that flow from Himalaya to the sea.   (22)

Rambha (*approaching Urvashi*): Congratulations, dear friend! You have enhanced both your son's glory as heir-apparent, and your own closeness to your husband!

Urvashi: This good fortune is for us all. (*Taking the boy's hand.*) Come, child, greet your senior mother.

King: Wait. We will all go together to that lady.

Narada (*to the king*):

This splendour, of the installation
as crown-prince, of your son Ayush,

reminds me of the consecration
by Indra of the god Kumara,[vi]
as divine army commander. (23)

King: The god Indra has favoured me.

Narada: What more can he do for you?

King: If Indra is pleased with me, what more can I ask for?
Still, may this too be:

(*Final verse.*)

Between those mutually opposite,
rare is their coming together,
like of the goddesses Shri and Sarasvati:
but for the good may there always be
of wealth and learning a unity. (24)

(*Exit all.*)

End of Act Five
End of the play Vikramorvashiyam

Notes

Introduction

(i) Velankar, H.D. (ed.), *The Vikramorvasiyam of Kalidasa*, Sahitya Akademi, New Delhi 1981, *n.b.* Editor's Introduction.

(ii) Radhakrishnan, S., General Introduction to *Critical Edition of Kalidasa's Work*, reproduced in Velankar (i) above; and Winternitz, M., *History of Indian Literature, vol. III*, (tr. from German by Subhadra Jha), Motilal Banarsidass Publishers, Delhi 1967.

(iii) Velankar, *The Vikramorvasiyam of Kalidasa*.

(iv) Winternitz, *History of Indian Literature*.

(v) Ibid. (footnote p. 247) and Barbara Stoler Miller, *Theatre of Memory: The Plays of Kalidasa*, Columbia University Press 1984, that included the translation of this play by David Gitomer.

(vi) Haksar, A.N.D., (tr.) *Raghuvamsam*, Penguin Random House India, Gurgaon 2016, Introduction, with these three verses and notes.

(vii) The first two are translations by A.N.D. Haksar, and the third by William Radice, respectively in their *Raghuvamsam*, Penguin Random House India, Gurgaon 2016 and *Selected Poems*, Penguin Books, New York 1985.

(viii) Miller, *Theatre of Memory*, translation by David Gitomer.

(ix) Velankar, *The Vikramorvasiyam of Kalidasa*, Editor's Introduction.

(x) Miller, *Theatre of Memory*, translation by David Gitomer.

(xi) Kale, M.R. (tr. & ed.), *Vikramorvasiyam of Kalidasa*, Delhi 1967.

(xii) Haksar, A.N.D. (tr.), *Raghuvamsam* and *Ritusamharam*, both of Kalidasa, Penguin Random House India, Gurgaon 2016 and 2018 respectively.

THE PLAY

ACT ONE

(i) Sthanu is another name for the Hindu god Shiva.

(ii) The name Urvashi is derived from *uru*, a Sanskrit word for the thigh. She was in legend created from the sage Narayana's thigh.

(iii) Shri is the goddess of prosperity, better known now as Lakshmi.

(iv) Kubera is the god of wealth, and lived on a Himalayan mountain peak.

(v) A reference to the king's ancestry.

(vi) Name of another Himalayan peak.

(vii) A reference to Indra, king of gods.

(viii) See (ii) above.

ACT TWO

(i) In myths, the bird *chataka* drank only drops of water falling from the sky.

(ii) A reference to the legend of the god Indra pursuing the ascetic lady Ahalya.

(iii) This name in Sanskrit here indicates a knot that cannot be undone.

(iv) Another epithet for the god Indra. He was also regarded as the lord of all apsaras.

(v) The legendary sweetheart of the wind.

ACT THREE

(i) A divine sage who propounded the sciences of drama and dance, Bharata was also the teacher of Urvashi.

(ii) A well-known name of the Hindu god Vishnu.

(iii) A reference to the Moon.

(iv) Another reference to the Moon as an ancestor of King Pururavas.

(v) A traditional omen of good luck.

(vi) A famous holy Himalayan peak still visited for pilgrimage.

(vii) A grass also used in ceremonies.

(viii) Shachi is the consort of Indra, king of the gods.

ACT FOUR

(i)   Also a name for the river Ganga in the hills.

(ii)   In Hindu mythology, the god Kumara is a son of Shiva, a celibate, and commander of divine army.

(iii)   In dramas, *Charchari* is a dance to a love song, described by the scholar Gitomer who is mentioned in the Notes to the introduction above.

(iv)   The tree Barrigtonia Acatungy, called Hijjal in Hindi.

(v)   *Kutilika* and *Mallaghati* are also dance styles other than that at (iii) above.

(vi)   In the name *chakravaka,* mentioned earlier, the syllable *chakra* also means a wheel.

(vii)   Well known tree Nauclea Cadamba with scented golden blossoms.

(viii) Well-known divine name, it also means 'The Wrathful One'.

ACT FIVE

(i)   A reference to the king's family.

(ii)   The tree Averrhoa Acida which has very pale leaves.

(iii)   See Act 3 note (vii). Paulomi is another name for Shachi.

(iv)   Narada is a divine sage and heavenly messenger.

(v)   This verse gives the lineage of King Pururavas.

(vi)   See Act 4 note (ii).

ALSO IN PENGUIN CLASSICS

Raghuvamsam
The Line of Raghu

Kalidasa

Translated by A.N.D. Haksar

Long considered as Kalidasa's greatest work, *Raghuvamsam* is an epic poem in classical Sanskrit. It recounts the legendary tales of the Raghu dynasty, whose scions include Rama, the hero of the Ramayana. In this majestic mahakavya, Kalidasa invokes the whole gamut of literary flavours, ranging from the erotic and the heroic to the tragic, horrific and peaceful. The forbears and the descendants of Rama are all brought to life. Within these pages we see the ideal couple, Dilipa and Sudakshina, their son Raghu's valour and generosity, the tragic love of Aja and Indumati, the travails of Dasaratha, the feats of Kusha and Atithi, and finally, the dynasty's downfall with Sudarshana and Agnivarna. Composed in nineteen cantos, this mesmerizing, lyrical and very accessible new translation of Raghuvamsam will continue to enthrall readers with its insights into ancient India, its land, people and seasons, and its social and cultural values that are still relevant today.

Ritusamharam
A Gathering of Seasons

Kalidasa
Translated by A.N.D. Haksar

Perhaps the most lively and exuberant of Kalidasa's extant works, *Ritusamharam* is a glorious ode to nature's bounty and the enduring emotional response it evokes in mankind as a whole. Recounted as a celebration of the passing seasons, it is a feast for the senses, capturing the myriad facets of love and longing in a kaleidoscope of sumptuous imagery: the mischievous moonlight that, like a pining lover, steals glances at sleeping maidens; the monsoon-bloated rivers that rush to the sea with a lustful urgency; the flame of lovemaking that is kindled anew at the onset of winter; the heady scent of mango blossoms that makes even the most unyielding of hearts quiver. Even animals, big and small, are swept into the playful pattern of the great poet's lyrical homage.

A.N.D. Haksar's supple and spirited translation is accompanied by an absorbing introduction and notes that shed further light on this extraordinary work.

Chanakya Niti
Verses on Life and Living

Translated by A.N.D. Haksar

Chanakya's numerous sayings on life and living—popularized in the wake of his successful strategy to put Chandragupta Maurya on the throne, if legend is to be believed—have been compiled in numerous collections and anthologies over time. This entire corpus was referred to as Chanakya Niti.

These aphorisms, which continue to be recalled and quoted in many parts of India, primarily deal with everyday living: with family and social surroundings, friends and enemies, wealth and knowledge, and the inevitable end of everything. They also advise on the good and bad in life, proper and improper conduct, and how to manage many difficult situations.

A.N.D. Haksar's wonderful translation also places this work into context, showing how these verses have endured in the popular imagination for so long.

My Shameless Heart
Love Lyrics of Amaru Shatakam

Amaru
Translated by A.N.D. Haksar

Amaru Shatakam is a collection of a hundred love lyrics that are
among the best known and most highly regarded such works in
the world of Sanskrit literature. Even though almost nothing is
known about Amaru himself, his reputation as the author of the
greatest Sanskrit love poetry has existed in literary record for over
a thousand years.

These ancient lyrics give vivid glimpses of human love in quite a
modern manner. The love they picture has physical, emotional as
well as social aspects. It is delightful and painful, and felt by women
as well as men. Each verse in the collection is sensitively drawn
portrait of love, sometimes in separation and loss and at other times
in desire and fulfilment.